Rita Zurke
246-7603

SO-AXN-944

✧ *Companions for the Journey* ✧

Praying with
Benedict

✧ *Companions for the Journey* ✧

Praying with Benedict

by
Katherine Howard, OSB

Saint Mary's Press
Christian Brothers Publications
Winona, Minnesota

✧   To God and you, the reader,   ✧
who live in God
and in whom God lives
in the Spirit of the Risen Christ.

With special thanks to Jana Preble; Jeremy Hall, OSB; Linda
Kulzer, OSB; and my Benedictine community and friends.

The publishing team for this book included Carl Koch, development editor; Laurie Berg Rohda, manuscript editor; Barbara Bartelson, typesetter;
Maurine R. Twait, art director; Elaine Kohner, illustrator; pre-press, printing,
and binding by the graphics division of Saint Mary's Press.

The acknowledgments continue on page 123.

Copyright © 1996 by Saint Mary's Press, 702 Terrace Heights, Winona, MN
55987-1320. All rights reserved. No part of this book may be reproduced by
any means without the written permission of the publisher.

Printed in the United States of America

Printing: 9 8 7 6 5 4 3 2 1

Year: 2004 03 02 01 00 99 98 97 96

ISBN 0-88489-379-0

✧ Contents ✧

✧ Foreword ✧

Companions for the Journey

Just as food is required for human life, so are companions. Indeed, the word *companions* comes from two Latin words: *com*, meaning "with," and *panis*, meaning "bread." Companions nourish our heart, mind, soul, and body. They are also the people with whom we can celebrate the sharing of bread.

Perhaps the most touching stories in the Bible are about companionship: the Last Supper, the wedding feast at Cana, the sharing of the loaves and the fishes, and Jesus' breaking of bread with the disciples on the road to Emmaus. Each incident of companionship with Jesus revealed more about his mercy, love, wisdom, suffering, and hope. When Jesus went to pray in the Garden of Olives, he craved the companionship of the Apostles. They let him down. But God sent the Spirit to inflame the hearts of the Apostles, and they became faithful companions to Jesus and to each other.

Throughout history, other faithful companions have followed Jesus and the Apostles. These saints and mystics have also taken the journey from conversion, through suffering, to resurrection. Just as they were inspired by the holy people who went before them, so too may you be inspired by these saints and mystics and take them as your companions on your spiritual journey.

The Companions for the Journey series is a response to the spiritual hunger of Christians. This series makes available the rich spiritual teachings of mystics and guides whose wisdom can help us on our pilgrimage. As you complete the last meditation in each volume, it is hoped that you will feel supported, challenged, and affirmed by a soul-companion on your spiritual journey.

The spiritual hunger that has emerged over the last twenty years is a great sign of renewal in Christian life. People fill retreat programs and workshops on topics in spirituality. The demand for spiritual directors exceeds the number available. Interest in the lives and writings of saints and mystics is increasing as people search for models of whole and holy Christian life.

Praying with Benedict

Praying with Benedict is more than just a book about Benedict's spirituality. This book seeks to engage you in praying in the way that Benedict did about issues and themes that were central to his experience. Each meditation can enlighten your understanding of his spirituality and lead you to reflect on your own experience.

The goal of *Praying with Benedict* is that you will discover Benedict's rich spirituality and integrate his spirit and wisdom into your relationship with God, with your brothers and sisters, and with your own heart and mind.

Suggestions for Praying with Benedict

Meet Benedict, a fascinating companion for your pilgrimage, by reading the introduction to this book, which begins on page 13. It provides a brief biography of Benedict and an outline of the major themes of his spirituality.

Once you meet Benedict, you will be ready to pray with him and to encounter God, your sisters and brothers, and yourself in new and wonderful ways. To help your prayer, here are some suggestions that have been part of the tradition of Christian spirituality:

Create a sacred space. Jesus said, "'Whenever you pray, go into your room and shut the door and pray to your [God] who is in secret; and your [God] who sees in secret will reward you'" (Matthew 6:6). Solitary prayer is best done in a place where you can have privacy and silence, both of which can be luxuries in the life of busy people. If privacy and silence are not possible, create a quiet, safe place within yourself, perhaps while riding to and from work, while sitting in line at the dentist's office, or while waiting for someone. Do the best you can, knowing that a loving God is present everywhere. Whether the meditations in this book are used for solitary prayer or with a group, try to create a prayerful mood with candles, meditative music, an open Bible, or a crucifix.

Open yourself to the power of prayer. Every human experience has a religious dimension. All of life is suffused with God's presence. So remind yourself that God is present as you begin your period of prayer. Do not worry about distractions. If something keeps intruding during your prayer, spend some time talking with God about it. Be flexible because God's Spirit blows where it will.

Prayer can open your mind and widen your vision. Be open to new ways of seeing God, people, and yourself. As you open yourself to the Spirit of God, different emotions are evoked, such as sadness from tender memories, or joy from a celebration recalled. Our emotions are messages from God that can tell us much about our spiritual quest. Also, prayer strengthens our will to act. Through prayer, God can touch our will and empower us to live according to what we know is true.

Finally, many of the meditations in this book will call you to employ your memories, your imagination, and the circumstances of your life as subjects for prayer. The great mystics and saints realized that they had to use all their resources to know God better. Indeed, God speaks to us continually and touches us constantly. We must learn to listen and feel with all the means that God has given us.

Come to prayer with an open mind, heart, and will.

Preview each meditation before beginning. After you have placed yourself in God's presence, spend a few moments previewing the readings and especially the reflection activities. Several reflection activities are given in each meditation because different styles of prayer appeal to different personalities or personal needs. **Note that each meditation has more reflection activities than can be done during one prayer period. Therefore, select only one or two reflection activities each time you use a meditation. Do not feel compelled to complete all the reflection activities.**

Read meditatively. Each meditation offers you a story about Benedict and a reading from his writings. Take your time reading. If a particular phrase touches you, stay with it. Relish its feelings, meanings, and concerns.

Use the reflections. Following the readings is a short reflection in commentary form, which is meant to give perspective to the readings. Then you are offered several ways of meditating on the readings and the theme of the prayer. You may be familiar with the different methods of meditating, but in case you are not, they are described briefly here:

✦ *Repeated short prayer or mantra:* One means of focusing your prayer is to use a *mantra,* or "prayer word." The mantra may be a single word or a short phrase taken from the readings or from the Scriptures. For example, the short prayer for meditation 1 in this book is "Here I am." Repeated slowly in harmony with your breathing, the mantra helps you center your heart and mind on one action or attribute of God.

✦ *Lectio divina:* This type of meditation is "divine studying," a concentrated reflection on the word of God or the wisdom of a spiritual writer. Most often in *lectio divina,* you will be invited to read one of the passages several times and then concentrate on one or two sentences, pondering their meaning for you and their effect on you. *Lectio divina* commonly ends with formulation of a resolution.

✦ *Guided meditation:* In this type of meditation, our imagination helps us consider alternative actions and likely consequences. Our imagination helps us experience new ways of seeing God, our neighbors, ourselves, and nature. When Jesus told his followers parables and stories, he engaged their imagination. In this book, you will be invited to follow guided meditations.

One way of doing a guided meditation is to read the scene or story several times, until you know the outline and can recall it when you enter into reflection. Or before your prayer time, you may wish to record the meditation on a tape recorder. If so, remember to allow pauses for reflection between phrases and to speak with a slow, peaceful pace and tone. Then, during prayer, when you have finished the readings and the reflection commentary, you can turn on your recording of the meditation and be led through it. If you find your own voice too distracting, ask a friend to make the tape for you.

✦ *Examen of consciousness:* The reflections often will ask you to examine how God has been speaking to you in your past and present experience—in other words, the reflections will ask you to examine your awareness of God's presence in your life.

✦ *Journal writing:* Writing is a process of discovery. If you write for any length of time, stating honestly what is on your mind and in your heart, you will unearth much about who you are, how you stand with your God, what deep longings reside in your soul, and more. In some reflections, you will be asked to write a dialog with Jesus or someone else. If you have never used writing as a means of meditation, try it. Reserve a special notebook for your journal writing. If desired, you can go back to your entries at a future time for an examen of consciousness.

✦ *Action:* Occasionally, a reflection will suggest singing a favorite hymn, going out for a walk, or undertaking some other physical activity. Actions can be meaningful forms of prayer.

Using the Meditations for Group Prayer

If you wish to use the meditations for community prayer, these suggestions may help:

✦ Read the theme to the group. Call the community into the presence of God, using the short opening prayer. Invite one or two participants to read one or both readings. If you use both readings, observe the pause between them.

✦ The reflection commentary may be used as a reading, or it can be deleted, depending on the needs and interests of the group.

✦ Select one of the reflection activities for your group. Allow sufficient time for your group to reflect, to recite a centering prayer or mantra, to accomplish a studying prayer (lectio divina), or to finish an examen of consciousness. Depending on the group and the amount of available time, you may want to invite the participants to share their reflections, responses, or petitions with the group.

✦ Reading the passage from the Scriptures may serve as a summary of the meditation.

✦ If a formulated prayer or a psalm is given as a closing, it may be recited by the entire group. Or you may ask participants to offer their own prayers for the closing.

Now you are ready to begin praying with Benedict, a faithful and caring companion on this stage of your spiritual journey. It is hoped that you will find him to be a true soul-companion.

CARL KOCH
Editor

Note: The author has used the most authentic source documents available. Because changing Benedict's and Gregory's words to make them inclusive would be intrusive in the extreme, the passages have not been altered.

✧ Introduction ✧

In recent years, fictitious Benedictine monks have made their way into the popular imagination. Brother Cadfael, the English Benedictine sleuth, unearths the truth and exposes villains in Ellis Peters' medieval mysteries set at the Abbey of Saint Peter and Saint Paul in Shrewsbury, England. Two bestsellers have been centered on Benedictine monasteries: *The Name of the Rose,* by Umberto Eco, and *Pillars of the Earth,* by Ken Follett.

Chant compositions of the medieval Benedictine abbess Hildegard of Bingen are being recorded and received with great enthusiasm. An album of Gregorian chant sung by Spanish Benedictine monks hit the top of the music charts recently, stimulating the production of recordings by other Benedictine communities.

Contemporary books on the Rule of Benedict and Benedictine life and prayer have taken their place in the spirituality sections of bookstores and have gained a wide readership.

Why all this fascination with Benedictines, their style of life, and their spiritual practice? The spirituality of the Rule of Benedict addresses in a profound and timeless way the desire for integrating work and prayer, hospitality and solitude, community and silence. In a world desperately seeking to find its balance, people have rediscovered Benedict's wisdom. It is as relevant now as it always has been, and may be needed now more than ever before.

Troubled Times

Benedict lived in a world searching for meaning, stability, and lasting values. The fifth and sixth centuries in Italy were times of great unrest, breakdown, and breakthrough, in some ways not unlike our own times. Internal weaknesses, natural disasters, and the invasions of migrating groups of peoples hastened the decline of the Roman Empire. The various nations moved about, conquered territory, and resettled, in the process changing political structures and relationships. The ever-present threat of disaster from war, plague, or failure of government lurked always just around the corner. In 476, just four years before Benedict's birth, Theodoric, the Gothic chieftain, deposed and replaced the last western Roman emperor. Great shifts were in progress.

The church was also changing. In 498, two rival candidates vied for the papacy. Though the church in Rome had influence, local church practices and worship varied. During the fourth and fifth centuries, the era of the great christological heresies, church councils made important decisions about the nature of Christ. However, theological conflicts about the way grace works in human life troubled the church in the fifth and sixth centuries.

Monasticism: Finding Peace in the Chaos

Monasticism was already a well-established tradition by the fifth and sixth centuries. Many women and men from the earliest Christian times had lived as celibate ascetics in the cities. By the third century many others had left urban areas for the desert to live in solitude, silence, celibacy, poverty, and prayer. Some of these monastic men and women lived alone; they were called hermits. Others lived in communities; these were the cenobites. While the causes of the monastic movement were complex, most of the early hermits and cenobites were inspired by the desire to give their lives and energy entirely to seeking God. In fact, the terms *monk* and *monastery* come from the Greek word *monos,* meaning "alone" or "single." Monastics focused their whole attention on God.

The official recognition of Christianity by Roman Emperor Constantine early in the fourth century prompted a large increase in the number of monks. With the persecution of Christians ended, monastic life became a substitute for martyrdom. Monastics wanted to be totally identified with Christ in the mystery of his dying and rising, just as the martyrs had been.

Nevertheless, monasticism could not remain untouched by social, ecclesiastical, and theological controversies. Some monastics fled to the desert to avoid the heavy taxes of the Roman Empire. Some tended toward Pelagianism, a heresy that exaggerated human effort in attaining salvation. Converted nomadic invaders, along with those from the well-established higher classes, began to be attracted to monastic life. These crosscurrents made monasticism diverse, sometimes to its benefit and sometimes to its harm.

Even so, in the midst of all the upheavals in church and society, monasticism became a leaven of stability. Within a radically changing world, it offered a way of life focused steadily on loving attention and response to the reality of God's presence and work through and in the Spirit of Christ.

Benedict became a part of this monastic movement. In fact, he synthesized its teaching and practice in a creative and lastingly effective way in his Rule. The way of life taught by Benedict provided and continues to provide for all Christians, not only monastics, a simple framework for growing in relationship with God.

Learning About Benedict

What we know about the events of Benedict's life comes from a short document, Book II of the *Dialogues* of Pope Gregory the Great, "The Life and Miracles of Saint Benedict," written in 593 and 594. The fundamental outline of Benedict's life given by Gregory is generally accepted as accurate because he was writing only about fifty years after the saint's death, and he names his major sources. Some knowledge about the way Benedict lived as a monk can also be surmised from the Rule he wrote. This Rule, his only written work, is the source for understanding Benedict's spirituality.

Book II of Gregory's *Dialogues*

Book II of the *Dialogues* is a kind of icon, a symbolic word painting of Benedict, intended to draw us into the theological and spiritual meaning of his life as Gregory saw it. Gregory was not writing biography or history in the contemporary sense. He was using stories to present his understanding of the significance of Benedict's life for the readers of his time.

Storytelling has always been an important way to celebrate and hand on the deep meaning of peoples' lives. We tell stories about great-grandparents, grandparents, parents, siblings, spouses, and friends. These stories are based in fact, but we often reorganize and embellish them so that they convey much more of the colorful character of their subjects than mere factual accounts could. To highlight some unique trait or accomplishment, we may even make up an entire story from pieces of actual events. Sometimes we use stories about others to communicate our own insights into life's values and dynamics. In a sense, this is what Gregory was doing.

Though Gregory's stories may be more carefully crafted and exhibit more literary polish than our homespun tales, similar purposes are accomplished. Adalbert de Vogüé, a contemporary Benedictine scholar and writer, says, "When we read the *Dialogues*, the right question is not, 'Is it true?' but 'What is it trying to say?'" (*The Life of Saint Benedict*, p. viii).

Miracles and prophecies abound in Gregory's account of the life of Benedict. Many of these are similar to the miracles and prophecies of the Scriptures and of the earlier lives of saints. Even if they have little, if any, foundation in fact, Gregory intended to show how Benedict, like those brought to mind by the stories, clearly manifested the presence and action of God in his life. It is impossible to know with certainty which of Benedict's miracles and prophecies can be traced back to some authentic event, which are embellished accounts, and which are not only interpreted in light of the Scriptures and the earlier lives of monks but are wholly borrowed from those sources.

Gregory's own comments in the *Dialogues* make it clear that his primary purpose was to present Benedict as a manifestation of Christ. After Gregory's account of Benedict's life at

Subiaco, Peter, Gregory's dialog partner, says that the miracles Benedict worked there remind him of Moses, Eliseus, Saint Peter, Elias, and David. Peter tells Gregory that this "man must have been filled with the spirit of all the just" (*Dialogues*, p. 25). Then Gregory offers this reply:

> Actually, Peter, blessed Benedict possessed the Spirit of only one Person, the Savior who fills the hearts of all the faithful by granting them the fruits of His Redemption. For St. John says of Him, "There is one who enlightens every soul born into the world; he was the true light." And again, "Of his fullness we have all received." (*Dialogues*, pp. 25–26)

Benedict's Story

The following facts about Benedict's life are generally agreed upon as well-founded in historical evidence. He was born at Nursia, Italy, about 480. As a young man he left home to go to Rome for a liberal education, but abandoned his studies there for life as a solitary monk near Subiaco. The discovery of the holy man by the local people and the desire of many to join him resulted in his founding of monasteries in that vicinity. After some years, Benedict, together with a group of his monks, moved farther south and established a monastery at Monte Cassino. There, Benedict wrote his Rule. He died at Monte Cassino about 547. The anniversary of his death is celebrated on 21 March.

To fill out the story, we must turn to Gregory's interpretation of Benedict's life, to the Rule, and to other historical sources.

Early Life in Nursia and Rome

"Some years ago," Gregory begins, "there lived a man who was revered for the holiness of his life." Not only does his name, the Latin word *benedictus*, mean "blessed," but Benedict "was blessed also with God's grace." Benedict's childhood is passed over in a single statement: "During his boyhood he showed mature understanding, and a strength of character far beyond his years kept his heart detached from every pleasure" (*Dialogues*, p. 1).

Nursia, Benedict's birthplace, is a small, ancient town in a rugged region about seventy miles northeast of Rome. One of the major Roman highways passed within twenty miles of the town. So Benedict and his family would not have been totally isolated from the major events and movements of the time.

Gregory says little about Benedict's family except that his father was a free man and that he had a sister, Scholastica. The family Gregory speaks of would have been at least moderately well-off because Benedict, like other young men of the same economic and social class, was sent to Rome to study the liberal arts. Because he was probably in his teens, Benedict's nurse, a faithful family servant, went with him to care for his needs.

Even though the Western Empire was crumbling, Rome remained a cultural mecca as well as an influential center of the church. In Rome, Benedict would have discovered the ancient treasures of classical civilization, and he would have walked in the footsteps of the Apostles and martyrs. Much about the intellectual, aesthetic, and spiritual richness of the life of a student was likely to have attracted him.

Call to Monastic Life

Benedict's desire for God reached a crisis point in Rome. While involved in his studies, he saw clearly that many of his fellow students spent their nights banqueting, vandalizing, drinking, and pursuing women, and their days competing for recognition by their teachers and fighting with rival schools—activities common to the youth of ancient Rome. Benedict feared that if he stayed there, Rome's allures would lead him to ruin.

His "desire to please God alone" won out. Turning decisively away from Rome's temptations, Benedict chose a way of life that would keep his heart fixed on God. He gave up his studies, abandoned Rome, his home, and his inheritance, and embraced the religious life. Gregory concluded, "He took this step, fully aware of his ignorance; yet he was truly wise, uneducated though he may have been" (*Dialogues*, p. 2).

Taking his nurse with him, Benedict set out toward the east and settled about thirty-five miles away from Rome at Affile where a group of dedicated Christians provided lodging for them near the local church. The support of these people must have been a comforting assurance of God's presence. However, here he began his interior battle with the temptation to vainglory.

Solitary Life at Subiaco

One day at Affile, Benedict's nurse had borrowed a tray from one of the local people to prepare wheat for making bread. It accidentally slipped from the edge of the table where she had set it and broke. When she burst into tears, her distress touched Benedict. He wept too, and prayed earnestly. The tray was miraculously mended. Word of the miracle spread rapidly around Affile. Out of admiration for Benedict, the townspeople hung the tray at the entrance of their church (*Dialogues*, p. 3).

Benedict took pleasure in the continuing admiration of the people. However, Gregory declares, Benedict wisely recognized the temptation to let his desire to do what was right be for the wrong reason. The pitfalls of too much acclaim made a great impression on Benedict. Deep within, his soul longed for more than the adulation of the crowds. Gregory says, "He wanted to spend himself laboring for God, not to be honored by the applause of [others]. So he stole away secretly from his nurse and fled to a lonely wilderness about thirty-five miles from Rome called Subiaco" (*Dialogues*, p. 4).

He sought more complete solitude as the antidote to overdependence on the approval of others. Like Christ, alone and tempted in the desert, Benedict chose to rely on God, not on any power or glory he could claim as his own.

A narrow cave in mountainous, wooded terrain became his home for three years. His whereabouts were known only to Romanus, a monk from a nearby monastery who clothed him with the monastic habit and secretly provided a portion of his own bread for Benedict, daily lowering it over a cliff on a rope in front of the cave's opening. Gregory says nothing else about Benedict's solitude during these three years but that he emerged from this hidden life as a person of great holiness.

As was customary for hermits, Benedict must have devoted long hours to reciting the psalms, reading and meditating on the rest of the Scriptures, and giving time to the prayer it inspired. He would have memorized much of the Bible, fixing the words in his mind and heart and letting them transform his life, something he had probably begun at Affile. Praying with the Scriptures would have occupied his time from dawn until well after noon when he would have his daily meal.

A number of hours every day had to be devoted to the work necessary to sustain him in this isolated place. From his cave high on the mountainside he no doubt would have had to climb down the craggy slopes to fetch water. Gathering edible fruit in season and cultivating a small plot of beans and barley may have also been part of his work.

A sheep or goatskin cloak and the rough wool habit, a kind of tunic not unlike those worn by the local shepherds, would have been his only clothing. These would have become progressively worn, tattered, and dirty during his solitary life at Subiaco.

His life in the mountains must have been hard and lonely. Facing himself in the daily solitude over a long period could have been overwhelming at times. Nonetheless, Benedict evidently learned to accept himself just as he was and, most of all, to constantly turn to God in trust. He embraced the solitude and persevered there until, as Gregory says, "at length the time came when almighty God wished to grant him rest from his toil and reveal Benedict's virtuous life to others. Like a shining lamp his example was to be set on a lampstand to give light to everyone in God's house" (*Dialogues*, p. 5).

One Easter Sunday, a priest who lived in the vicinity discovered Benedict. Soon after that, local shepherds came to him to listen as he spoke about the Good News. Even though he wore ragged skins and looked wild, they recognized his holiness. Benedict instructed the local people about the spiritual life, and they provided him with food in return.

Founder and Abbot

Disciples came to Benedict, placing themselves under his guidance, "for now that he was free from these temptations he was ready to instruct others in the practice of virtue" (*Dialogues*, p. 8).

Soon a group of local monks asked him to be their abbot. They had been living according to their own whims and fancies. At first he resisted the invitation because he doubted their willingness to live as he was living. Because of their persistence, he reluctantly accepted. Benedict's reforms proved distasteful to them, and they became increasingly sullen and resentful. Finally they tried to murder him with poisoned wine. He miraculously escaped.

Without succumbing to discouragement in his failure to bring about any change in them or anger at their attempt to murder him, Benedict knew that further efforts would be in vain. As a result, he returned to the life of a hermit.

Benedict was not left alone in his solitude for long. Gregory comments:

> As Benedict's influence spread over the surrounding countryside because of his signs and wonders, a great number of men gathered around him to devote themselves to God's service. Christ blessed his work and before long he had established twelve monasteries there, with an abbot and twelve monks in each of them (*Dialogues*, p. 16).

Benedict, though, was not universally loved. Florentius, a local priest, "envious as the wicked always are of the holiness in others which they are not striving to acquire themselves" (*Dialogues*, p. 22), not only sent him a poisoned loaf of bread to kill him but, when that failed, sent seven women to dance in the monastery garden to seduce the monks. Benedict decided to leave Subiaco with a small group of monks to find a new home.

Monte Cassino

Benedict and his disciples settled about seventy miles south of Rome at Monte Cassino. Clearing land of briers and rocks so gardens, fields, and orchards could be planted and constructing the abbey's buildings and surrounding wall out of large stones demanded perseverance and hard work.

As abbot at Monte Cassino, Benedict not only supervised the building of the monastery's walls and gardens, but also the growth of the monks' spiritual life. According to Gregory, Benedict's prayerfulness gave Benedict such clarity of vision that he was able to see into people's hearts, and his compassion guided him to use this gift for each person's good.

One time, for example, when some of the monks had to go out for an assigned duty that kept them busy until late in the day, they stopped for dinner at the home of a woman in the area before returning to the monastery, even though this was not permitted. When Benedict inquired about where they ate, they replied, "'Nowhere'" (*Dialogues*, p. 32). Of course, Benedict already knew exactly what they had done, even what they had eaten and drunk. He proceeded to recount all the details of their side trip. Shocked and frightened, their hearts were moved to repentance, which Benedict readily confirmed with his loving pardon.

During Benedict's life, the monastery remained an oasis of God's peaceable power. Gregory's account indicates that Benedict and his monks received all those who came, whether they were barbarians or descendants of longtime Roman citizens, local farmers and shepherds, or nobles and clerics. The poor received help, even at the possible expense of lack of provisions for the monks themselves.

The Rule of Benedict

Benedict wrote his Rule at Monte Cassino, probably completing it toward the end of his life. It was his legacy to his community, his synthesis of the wisdom gained from a lifetime not only of study and reflection on earlier monastic sources, but of practical experience. Reading this succinct little document, according to Gregory himself, is the best way to understand Benedict's "life and character," for "his life could not have differed from his teaching" (*Dialogues*, p. 74).

Benedict's Rule incorporates the teaching of many other monastic and ecclesial sources. Like all monastic Rules, the Rule of Benedict is not a spiritual or theological treatise, but rather a compendium of practical directives, a concretization of Scripture as a guide for daily life. Scripture has always been the primary "Rule," the source of life, for monastics as for all Christians. It is not surprising, then, that Benedict invites us in the Prologue to "set out on this way, with the Gospel for our guide" (Timothy Fry, ed., *The Rule of St. Benedict in Latin and English with Notes*, Prologue 21).

Modern readers might find life according to the Rule strict, and it contains some practices, such as physical punishment for serious faults, that reflect sixth-century culture. Even so, moderation and balance are its hallmarks.

Daily Life at Monte Cassino

In Benedict's Rule, everything had its time: the needs of body and spirit—time for sleep, community meals, and attention to community and individual concerns; time for prayer, work, reading, and study. Benedict took the attitude that the way one lived and worked—respectfully and lovingly attentive to God and others—was at least as important as what one accomplished.

In Benedict's monasteries, everything had its place too: an oratory for prayer, a refectory for meals, dormitories for sleeping, a guesthouse for visitors, fields and gardens for growing food, and so on. The material as well as the spiritual components of life were respected and treated with care.

The monks held all material goods in common. Proper care was to be taken of everything so that the next person to use anything would find it in good condition. The monks even looked after the used clothing still good enough to be given to the poor.

For Benedict and his community, the time of rising and going to bed, and the length of the equally divided "hours" in each day would have varied according to the seasons. Benedict and all the monks, except those who were too old, young, or sick, got up before dawn to come to vigils, the first "hour" of the divine office, or liturgy of hours. After an interval for individual prayerful reading of Scripture, he returned to the oratory with the monks for lauds and prime when the sun rose. After that he probably gathered the community together in what came to be called "chapter," to assign or adjust their daily work assignments and to make other necessary announcements. He no doubt would have concluded with some short instruction about their rule of life based in the word of God.

Following this, Benedict and the others went to do the necessary work. Some might have gone to the fields, the scriptorium, the kitchen, or to do carpentry and maintenance work. Others might have gone to teach the young monks, or to care for the sick in the infirmary, and the visitors in the guest quarters.

Benedict himself may have gone to his room to listen to the concerns and prayers of individual monks. The personal, spiritual welfare of each community member was his top priority. Some days he probably would have needed to study and write. Sometimes there would have been conferences with the guests who were waiting to converse with and be instructed by him. And there was always the task of overseeing the work of those to whom he had delegated authority. The financial and legal affairs of the monastery had to be attended to. As abbot, he was ultimately responsible for everything.

Benedict approached the daily discipline of work with moderation. If the demands in any particular area were especially heavy, he assigned extra help so that no one was overburdened. During the hot months of summer, time was allowed for a siesta after the noon meal.

The work time of the monastery was, moreover, well-punctuated with time for brief community prayer at the third, sixth, and ninth hours of the day. The monks also had time for individual prayerful reading, in the morning during the summer and Lent, later in the afternoon during the winter months. The day concluded with prayer—vespers toward sunset and compline just before retiring for the night. Benedict knew from his own experience that this fostered the unceasing prayer to which the Gospel exhorts all Christians.

The main meal was served at noon in the summer and in midafternoon after the middle of September. During Lent they ate toward evening. On days and during seasons when they were not fasting, they also had a light supper. Everything was done by daylight. In addition to bread and any available fruits and vegetables, two cooked dishes were served in order to provide for individual needs.

A moderate and humane atmosphere in the monastery was assured not only by the schedule and regulations set up by the Rule, but also by the pastoral approach of Abbot Benedict. As abbot, he represented Christ in a special way in the monastery, teaching only what Christ would teach, instructing not only by word, but even more by example.

The Triumph of Love

Becoming fully convinced of the superiority of love over law seems to have been something Benedict learned from his sister, Scholastica, according to Gregory. His story has it that Scholastica had become a nun when she was very young. Every year she came to visit her brother at a house the monastery owned not too far from the monastery gate.

On one particular visit they were so engrossed in their conversation that they did not have their meal together until it was getting dark. Finally, noticing the late hour, Scholastica said, "'Please do not leave me tonight, brother. Let us keep on talking about the joys of heaven till morning.'" Alarmed at the suggestion of departing from the usual monastery regulation, Benedict replied, "'What are you saying, sister? . . . You know I cannot stay away from the monastery'" (*Dialogues*, pp. 67–68).

Scholastica folded her hands on the table and rested her head upon them in earnest prayer. When she looked up again, a sudden burst of lightning and thunder accompanied a downpour that prevented Benedict and his companions from setting foot outside the door.

Evidently upset that he would have to break the monastery rule, Benedict complained bitterly saying, "'God forgive you, sister! . . . What have you done?'" (*Dialogues*, p. 68). Scholastica simply answered, "'When I appealed to you, you would not listen to me. So I turned to my God and He heard my prayer'" (*Dialogues*, p. 68). Humbled by his realization "that her influence was greater than his, since hers was the greater love" (*Dialogues*, p. 69), Benedict offered no protest.

Benedict's Death

A week before he died, Gregory comments, Benedict gave directions for his grave to be readied. A violent fever grew worse daily. On the sixth day, he had his disciples carry him into the chapel where he received the Eucharist. Then, leaning his weak body on the strong arms of his brothers, he stood with his hands raised to heaven and, as he prayed, he breathed his last.

The Spirituality of the Rule of Benedict

The spirituality of the Rule of Benedict is basic Christian spirituality. The Rule establishes a way of life that fosters the human return to God through and in Christ by the power of the Holy Spirit.

Seeking God

In the spirituality of the Rule, God is primary. The most important criterion for acceptance into the community is whether one "truly seeks God" (*Rule*, 58.7). The structure of life is designed to heighten and refine awareness of God's presence at all times.

Christ Awareness

Through and in Christ the Divine Presence is with us continually: Christ in Scripture and in ourselves during times of prayer and work, Christ in one another, Christ in the guest, and Christ in the poor. Christ daily invites us to "true and eternal life" (*Rule*, Prologue 17). His love for us and ours for him "must come before all else" (*Rule*, 4.21). The goal of the life described by the Rule is the goal of every Christian life: transformation in Christ.

Transformation in the Holy Spirit

Christ transforms us "by the Holy Spirit" (*Rule*, 7.70), with our cooperation, bringing us to "that *perfect love* of God which *casts out fear*" (*Rule*, 7.67 quoting 1 John 4:18).

Harmonious Living

The Rule aids transformation in the Spirit by helping Benedictine monastics to bring all these elements of Christian life into harmony or balance:

Listening: The Rule fosters listening and responding to the word of God. Participation in liturgy of hours and *lectio divina*—holy reading—alternate with work and the other components of community life: meals, meetings, conversation, and time alone.

Silence: An atmosphere of silence cultivates responsive listening so that the word heard during times devoted explicitly to prayer can be repeated, and come to repeat itself in the heart, during the rest of the day.

Obedience: Those who learn to "cherish Christ above all" come to obey naturally (*Rule*, 5.2). Their identification with him in love motivates them to live in accord with God's will. Ready obedience in external matters is an expression of this interior disposition.

Humility: The more we turn our attention to the divine presence, the more we are drawn into a kind of downward mobility, eventually welcoming joyfully the truth that God is God and we are not. At the point where the full realization of our poverty and weakness sinks in, the joy of God's presence in all of life, and our absolute and willing dependence on that, breaks through.

Stability in community: Enduring commitment to Christ is essential if inner transformation is to take place. Some stability in place and relationships is necessary to support this commitment.

Mutual love in the common life: Holding all goods in common, serving and loving one another with all our "weaknesses of body or behavior, and earnestly competing in obedience to one another" (*Rule*, 72.5–6) are the ordinary ways of expressing loving attention to Christ and living in union with him.

Hospitality: The Christocentric spirituality of the Rule is also made explicit by Benedict in his mandates about receiving guests as though they were Christ himself.

Trust: Benedict advises us to place our trust hope "in God alone" (*Rule*, 4.41) and "never lose hope in God's mercy" (*Rule*, 4.74).

Compassion: The compassion of Christ, the Good Shepherd, is the model for authority in the Rule. Mercy is always to *"triumph over judgment"* (*Rule*, 64.10 quoting James 2:13).

Contemporary Value
of Benedict's Life and Rule

The central message of Gregory's "The Life and Miracles of Saint Benedict" and of the *Rule of Benedict* is that God is present and active in our world and in each of us, always waiting for our awareness and response. All of us have monastic hearts, that is, hearts that long for God alone. Only when we hear and attend seriously to our longing and become firmly grounded in the Divine Presence can we make the decisions and take the action that is truly good for us, our families, nations, and earth.

The principles and practices of the Rule can be adapted to and be helpful for all Christians in developing this groundedness in the Divine Presence. The Rule makes it plain that God is with us through and in Christ and the Holy Spirit in the daily events of life. Neither the poor nor the rich, the old nor the young, neither those in authority nor those subject to authority are excluded from the love of God. For God's presence to be effective in our life requires only our consent and cooperation.

To pray with Benedict is to listen and respond "with the ear of [our] heart" (*Rule*, Prologue 1) to God's word, allowing the transforming power of God's love in the Spirit of Christ to make us loving women and men.

[Then] as we progress in this way of life and in faith, we shall run on the path of God's commandments, our hearts overflowing with the inexpressible delight of love. Never swerving from his instructions . . . , but faithfully observing his teaching . . . until death, we shall through patience share in the sufferings of Christ that we may deserve also to share in his kingdom. Amen. (*Rule*, Prologue 49–50)

✧ Meditation 1 ✧

Thirsting for the Living God

Theme: Desire for God was central in Benedict's life because it was his response to God's desire for him. The same desire lives deep in each of our hearts—the echo of God's longing for us.

Opening prayer: Gracious and loving God, stir up your Spirit within me so that I may realize the infinite depths of your love for me. Fill me with desire for you in response to your love.

About Benedict

When Benedict was a young man studying in Rome, he felt a compelling attraction to respond wholeheartedly to God. A strong sense of God's goodness and love in his life moved him to desire God above everything else.

We can imagine the frivolous life of his fellow students in Rome: banqueting and drinking by night, competing for the adulation of teachers and struggling for power and success in their academic pursuits by day. All this left Benedict feeling disillusioned, but also afraid that he could get caught up in this kind of life. He wanted no pleasure, no security, no power to substitute for God. "Even while still living in the world, free to enjoy all it had to offer, he saw how empty it was and turned from it without regret" (*Dialogues*, p. 1). His desire was "to please God alone" (*Dialogues*, p. 2).

Moved by his desire to seek God alone, Benedict retired, first to live with a rural Christian community and then in a cave near Subiaco. His outer separation from his former companions and way of life brought him more deeply into his inner human struggle for freedom from domination by esteem, pleasure, power, and control. In this battle, he placed his trust in God, desiring only God's will, a life in love with God.

He learned to love his life of solitude, but a time came, Gregory tells us, "when almighty God wished to grant him rest from his toil and reveal Benedict's virtuous life to others. Like a shining lamp his example was to be set on a lampstand to give light to everyone in God's house" (*Dialogues*, p. 5).

Benedict's desire for God, however, always remained his single focus. Even though God's work in his life did not allow him to live in the wilderness very long, he continued to live "in the presence of his heavenly Father" (*Dialogues*, p. 11). He lived so much in union with God that Gregory often refers to him as "the man of God."

Pause: Reflect on the ways you have known God's desire for you and your desire for God.

Benedict's Words

Seeking his [worker] in a multitude of people, the Lord calls out to him and lifts his voice again: *Is there anyone here who yearns for life and desires to see good days?* (Ps 33[34]:13). If you hear this and your answer is "I do," God then directs these words to you: If you desire true and eternal life, *keep your tongue free from vicious talk and your lips from all deceit; turn away from evil and do good; let peace be your quest and aim* (Ps 33[34]:14–15). Once you have done this, my *eyes will be upon* you *and* my *ears will listen* for your *prayers; and even before you ask me, I will say* to you: *Here I am* (Isa 58:9). What, dear brothers [and sisters], is more delightful than this voice of the Lord calling to us? See how the Lord in . . . love shows us the way of life." (*Rule*, Prologue 14–20)

Reflection

Benedict's desire for God was the primary motivation of his life. This desire is the echo of God's longing for us. To speak so movingly of God's desire for us as Benedict does in the Prologue of the Rule, often in the words of the Scriptures, he must have experienced it deeply. He was aware that every day, and every moment of the day, light is coming to us from God; God's voice is calling out to us in many ways saying: Do not harden yourself, but "listen . . . with the ear of your heart" (*Rule*, Prologue 1).

God's light is always showing us and God's voice is always telling us: "I love you. I long for you. Turn to me. I will give you true and lasting life. Pay attention to the longing for me in your heart. Your longing echoes my desire for you."

God's love, God's light, God's voice touch us in many different ways. We hear God speak in Scripture and in liturgy. We see God in another's eyes, hear God in another's voice. Whenever we are touched by love, beauty, or truth, we are in some way touched by God. Sometimes we are touched by God directly from within.

Benedict responded to God's loving touch by seeking out solitude in a cave for three years. Though that response is not possible or appropriate for most of us, our interior surrender to God in the solitude of our heart in prayer can be just as complete and effective.

✧ Slowly reread the passage in the "Benedict's Words" section quoted from the Prologue of the *Rule of Benedict*. Reread it several times if necessary. Stop at the word or phrase that speaks to your heart. Let yourself repeat the phrase interiorly as long as it attracts you. If you are drawn into silence just rest in God's presence.

✧ Take a minivacation of several hours on a day when you are rested. Or, if you only have small snatches of time, spread this exercise out over a span of short sessions.

With an album of pictures from various times of your life and a pen or a pencil and a notebook in hand, find a quiet room or corner where you can be alone without the likelihood of interruption. Settle yourself comfortably in a way that will help you stay alert and interiorly open. Remind yourself of God's loving presence within you, and ask that these hours be blessed.

Now, while looking at the pictures, remember each of these times of your life. Recall one or two important ways during your life in which you experienced God's love, God's desire for you, or your desire for God. Write a description of both the exterior events and your inner experience: how you felt, what you thought, and how you responded. Comment on the way these experiences have affected your life.

Conclude by writing a prayer expressing your gratitude to God for the love received and your desire to be with God in love now.

✧ Settle down quietly and slowly repeat aloud or in your heart the following verse:

> O God, you are my God whom I eagerly seek;
> for you my flesh longs and my soul thirsts
> like the earth, parched, lifeless, and without water.
> I have gazed toward you in the sanctuary
> to see your power and your glory.
> For your love is better than life;
> my lips shall glorify you.
>
> (Psalm 63:1–3)

Write the verse on a small card or piece of paper and carry it with you today. Take it out and pray it whenever you have a little in-between time.

✧ Make a list of the five things you most want in life—not the things you think you should want or what you think others might think you should want—but the things you really want. Then ponder these questions:

✦ Is it God I am seeking in and beyond these things?

✦ Am I grasping after them compulsively as substitutes for God?

Then close your eyes. Rest your hands with the palms up on your lap. In your imagination, hold the five things you most desire in your hands. Ponder them. When you are ready, turn your palms down. If you need to let go of any of these things and your desire for them, imagine dropping them into Christ's hands, letting go of them and their hold over you. If you are unable to do that, do not try to force yourself. Only pray trustingly that you may know God's love more deeply, and ask for God's grace to let go in God's time.

✧ Desire for God gives us eyes to see the Divine Presence in the beauties of nature. Make a visit out in nature. Simply pay attention to a tree, a flower, a plant, or some other natural creation.

Express the longing for God this stirs up in you in whatever words come to you or in a wordless gesture like lifting your head and opening your arms or by dancing joyfully! Or perhaps your response is completely interior. Open your heart fully in desire, welcome, wonder, awe, and thanksgiving. Rest in the presence of infinite beauty and love.

God's Word

> Like the deer that yearns
> for running streams,
> so my soul is yearning
> for you, my God.
> My soul is thirsting for God, the living God.
> When can I enter to see the face of God?
>
> (Psalm 42:1–2)

Closing prayer: Gracious God, thank you for renewing my confidence in your love for me, and for increasing my desire for you. In all life's gifts and losses, keep my inner eye open to the light that comes from you, and keep the ear of my heart alert and longing to hear your voice saying, "Here I am."

The Love of Christ

Theme: Christ unites us in love with himself and with one another in God. That is the central experience of Christianity. Benedict's life and Rule put the love of Christ before all else.

Opening prayer: O Christ, friend and lover of all, life of our life, stir up your love in my heart. Show me how to live in union with you so that I may love God and others with humility and sincerity.

About Benedict

The inner power of Benedict's life both as a solitary and as a founder and abbot was the love of Christ. "Christ blessed his work," as Gregory asserts (*Dialogues,* p. 16). Sometimes Christ's love manifested itself in confrontation and othertimes in tenderness. Gregory tells one tale of Benedict's tough love that hints at Christ's driving the moneychangers from the Temple.

Benedict did not give up on a restless monk who would not, or could not, pray. After the psalmody, all the monks entered into silent prayer, all except this monk who left the oratory "and passed the time aimlessly at whatever happened to interest him." Repeated corrections by his own abbot, Pompeianus, had no effect. Even after he was sent to Benedict and "received a stern rebuke for his folly," he reformed for only two days (*Dialogues,* p. 17).

But Benedict persisted in concern for his brother. He "sent word that he was coming over himself to see that the monk mended his ways" (*Dialogues,* p. 17). His keenly developed spiritual powers showed him that an evil spirit was taking advantage of the monk's restlessness and dragging him away from prayer.

After two days of prayer, Benedict came upon the distracted monk loitering outside, having avoided prayers again. Realizing that this attack by the tempter called for an even more stern approach, Benedict whacked the monk with his staff, driving the evil spirit away for good. "From then on the monk remained quietly at prayer like the rest. . . . It was as if that ancient enemy had been struck by the blow himself and was afraid to domineer over the monk's thoughts any longer" (*Dialogues,* p. 18).

Another miracle that Gregory attributes to Benedict's union with the loving Christ happened this way. One time Benedict, though inside at the time, knew immediately that the young monk Placid had toppled over into the lake while filling a bucket. He was in danger of drowning. Out of love, Benedict cried out, "Hurry, Brother Maurus! The boy who just went down for water has fallen into the lake, and the current is carrying him away" (*Dialogues,* p. 20). Maurus ran until he had grabbed the boy by the hair and dashed with him back to shore. Only then did he realize that he had walked on water!

On another occasion a Goth, a recently received member of Benedict's monastery, was working energetically clearing land for a garden. This poor man, as a rather new and unwelcome arrival in Italy, would have been at the bottom of the social ladder. In his vigorous effort to clear away a patch of briers near the lake, the brushhook flew off the handle of his tool and landed in deep water. With no way to retrieve it and terrified at what he had done, he ran and told Maurus, apologizing for his carelessness. When Maurus told Benedict about the accident he left everything at once, went to the Goth, took the handle of the tool, and thrust the end of it into the water. The iron blade was at once restored to the handle. As he gave the tool back to the monk, Benedict said, "Continue with your work now. There is no need to be upset" (*Dialogues*, p. 20).

Hearing these instances of Benedict's charity, Peter, the person with whom Gregory is sharing Benedict's story, exclaims in amazement, "'This man must have been filled with the spirit of all the just.'" This gave Gregory the chance to add this important comment: "'Actually, Peter, blessed Benedict possessed the Spirit of only one Person, the Savior who fills the hearts of all the faithful by granting them the fruits of His Redemption'" (*Dialogues*, pp. 25–26). The love of Christ filled Benedict's heart and motivated his loving deeds.

Pause: In what ways has Christ's love for you become apparent to you in your life? In what ways has Christ's love in you touched others?

Benedict's Words

Every page of Benedict's Rule, from beginning to end, is filled with the love of Christ: Christ in the abbot and community, Christ in Scripture, Christ in the sick, Christ in the guest.

The Rule is written for those who "are ready to give up [their] own will, once and for all, and . . . to do battle for the true King, Christ the Lord" (*Rule*, Prologue 3). He it is to whom we pray most earnestly "to bring . . . to perfection" the good works we begin (*Rule*, Prologue 4). And it is "with Christ's help" that we "keep this little rule . . . written for beginners" (*Rule*, 73.8).

Benedict admonishes:

> Your way of acting, should be different from the world's way; the love of Christ must come before all else. You are not to act in anger or nurse a grudge. Rid your heart of all deceit. Never give a hollow greeting of peace or turn away when someone needs your love. Bind yourself to no oath lest it prove false, but speak the truth with heart and tongue. (*Rule*, 4.20–28)

> Nothing is to be preferred to Christ on whom we depend to "bring us all together to everlasting life." (*Rule*, 72.11)

Reflection

Benedict's love of Christ did come before all else. As a result, like all holy women and men, he acted as Christ would. When he wrote the Rule, Benedict was aware of Christ's presence and tried to compose monastic life so that members of the community would live according to the way of Christ. They were to listen to Christ, obey him, cherish him, depend on him, suffer with him, rejoice with him, and love him. Only by being deeply touched by Christ's love could they learn to love.

In the love and protection of his family, Benedict must have felt Christ's love. It guided him in his discouragement and disillusionment with his fellow students in Rome. It did not leave him in the mixture of excitement, grief, and loneliness he must have felt as he left his nurse and his friends to find a place of solitude. But, according to Gregory, it was during Benedict's testing and purification in the cave at Subiaco that Christ's love was firmly and fully established as the center of his life.

For all believers in Christ, the goal and fulfillment of life is to be able to say like Benedict and Paul, "'It is no longer I who live, but it is Christ who lives in me'" (Galatians 2:20).

✧ Take your Bible and find a quiet spot, if possible, where you feel safe and at home, a place where you will not be interrupted. In words or gestures, express your faith in Christ present with and in you, and in his love for you. Begin to read slowly through one of the Gospels, attending with your heart more than your mind to the ways Christ is manifesting his love for you now. When you are touched by his love, stop and tell him, or just let yourself be drawn silently into that love.

✧ Read through the "Benedict's Words" section again. This time stop to look at the various experiences of your daily life in the light of Benedict's focus on Christ.
✦ How do you turn to him for help?
✦ In what people are you especially aware of his presence and action?

✦ How has he touched you in Scripture, in liturgy, and in personal prayer?

✦ When have you experienced as your suffering and joy part of his dying and rising?

When you have concluded your reflections, talk to him sincerely and honestly about your responses or sit in silence with him.

✧ Reread the "About Benedict" section. Think about how Christ has touched others through you.

✦ When have you exercised "tough love" in dealing with someone you have some responsibility for?

✦ When have you listened to another at a depth that was beyond your usual natural capacity?

✦ When have you been heedless of obstacles in working for another's good?

✦ When have you set aside self-centered concern and attention to your own affairs to pray or work earnestly for another's welfare?

✦ When have you gone out of your way to help a frightened or alienated person?

Take some time to thank Christ for his work in these particular ways in you.

✧ Pray repeatedly today Paul's words to the Galatians: "'It is no longer I who live, but it is Christ who lives in me.'" As you pray it, ask for the grace you need to make this more and more true.

✧ Sing your favorite hymn of praise to Christ.

God's Word

Who will separate us from the love of Christ? Will hardship, or distress, or persecution, or famine, or nakedness, or peril, or sword? As it is written,

> "For your sake we are being killed all day long;
> we are accounted as sheep to be slaughtered."

No, in all these things we are more than conquerors through him who loved us. For I am convinced that neither death, nor life, nor angels, nor rulers, nor things present, nor things to come, nor powers, nor height, nor depth, nor anything else in all creation, will be able to separate us from the love of God in Christ Jesus our Lord. (Romans 8:35–39)

Closing prayer: Thank you, Christ Jesus, for opening the eyes and ears of my heart to your love. Stay with me as I go out from this place so that I can bring your love to others.

Seven Times a Day Have I Praised You

Theme: God's goodness and love is continually being manifested in our life through and in the Spirit of Christ. Grateful praise of God is always fitting.

Opening prayer: Ever present God of goodness and love, your mysterious ways are beyond my comprehension. Touch me now in the Spirit of Christ, filling my mind, my heart, and my mouth with praise of you.

About Benedict

"Lord, open my lips and my mouth shall proclaim your praise (Ps 50[51]:17)" (*Rule,* 9.1) were the first words on Benedict's and his brothers' lips every morning of their life in the monasteries at Subiaco and Monte Cassino. Before these words sung by the community rolled gently out over the valley each day, no words were spoken. The only sounds were the few gentle murmurs of encouragement by the eager to the weary during the shuffle of rising quickly in the dimly lighted sleeping quarters as all made haste to get to the oratory on time. Perhaps some of the lay guests who were staying with them and

an occasional curious local farmer or secretly pious shepherd might join the monks there.

That call to worship opened vigils, the first hour of the divine office, or liturgy of hours, which started Benedict's and his monks' day before a hint of the dawn, long before in the winter! Led by a cantor, first those on one side of the room, then those on the other, chanted the verse wholeheartedly.

In the monastery at Subiaco the distant rushing and gurgling of the Anio River from the valley below and the gentle sound of the wind in the pines provided a natural accompaniment as the monks stood and recited or chanted from memory the psalms that followed. Sometimes the cantor led a sung refrain before and after certain psalms. And they always sang a Scripture-based hymn, one of those attributed to Saint Ambrose and growing in popularity. After each psalm they paused for silent prayer. An occasional screech or howl of some wild bird or animal in the craggy hills or the bleating of restless sheep provided the only counterpoint to the simple chants, the solemn recitation, and the silent interludes.

At the designated time, all would be seated in readiness to listen to the word of God. One of the monks rising from his place would reverently approach the reader's stand, take up the manuscript of the book of the Bible they were currently reading, and then proclaim the assigned text to the assembled community. Sometimes he would read from one of the "explanations of Scripture by reputable and orthodox catholic [writers]" (*Rule*, 9.8). After each reading, all joined in a sung response which concluded with a "Glory be to the Father." "As soon as the cantor [began] to sing 'Glory be to the Father,' . . . all the monks [rose] from their seats in honor and reverence for the Holy Trinity." Then more psalmody. After a versicle, a short Scripture verse, vigils concluded with a litany to which all responded "Lord, have mercy" (*Rule*, 9.7).

Seven other times during the day, as soon as the bell sounded, Benedict and his brothers immediately left what they were doing to come together for the divine office, which he called the Work of God.

After an interval that followed vigils, the monks returned to the oratory as day was breaking, to sing lauds (morning praise), sometimes called matins. Its focus was pure praise of God for the return of the light of creation, the rising sun, but especially for the Risen Son of God, the Divine Light of creation and redemption, whose presence was their life and joy. As the sun was setting, they gathered for vespers (evening prayer) in gratitude and praise for the goodness and light of the day, especially for Christ the Light who would now keep them through the night.

The day's work was regularly punctuated with the shorter hours of the divine office. Before they went to their daily assigned tasks they chanted prime. At midmorning they immediately stopped what they were doing when they heard the signal and prayed terce; at noon, sext; and in midafternoon, none. Compline prepared them for the night's rest.

These eight periods of singing or reciting the psalms together, listening to the word of God proclaimed, and responding in song and silent prayer was the basic structure of every one of Benedict's days. Sundays were special because the office was more festive. It was also most likely the occasion either for Benedict and his brothers to join the local people in their celebration of Eucharist or to celebrate Eucharist with their guests and perhaps some local shepherds at the monastery with a visiting priest presiding.

Week after week, month after month, season after season, year after year, on good days and bad, the praise of God was on Benedict's mind, in his heart, and on his lips.

Pause: What place does praising God have in your life?

Benedict's Words

The Prophet says: *Seven times a day have I praised you* (Ps 118[119]:164). We will fulfill this sacred number of seven if we satisfy our obligations of service at Lauds, Prime, Terce, Sext, None, Vespers and Compline, for it was of these hours during the day that he said: *Seven times a day have I praised you* (Ps 118[119]:164). Concerning Vigils, the same Prophet says: *At midnight I arose to give you praise* (Ps 118[119]:62). Therefore, we should *praise* our Creator *for his just judgments* at these times: Lauds, Prime, Terce, Sext, None, Vespers and Compline; and *let us arise at night to give* him *praise* (Ps 118[119]:164,62). (*Rule,* 16)

On hearing the signal for an hour of the divine office, the monk will immediately set aside what he has in hand and go with utmost speed, yet with gravity and without giving occasion for frivolity. Indeed, nothing is to be preferred to the Work of God. (*Rule,* 43.1–2)

Reflection

Offering praise should be a spontaneous and natural response to God's bountiful goodness. Most Christians cannot stop their work at regular intervals during the day or rise earlier to sing God's praises like Benedict and his followers. All can include psalms and hymns of praise in their morning and evening prayer and sometimes at other intervals during the day.

Benedict calls liturgy the Work of God. It is the symbolic celebration of the work God is doing in us and in our world. God is present and at work in us in the Spirit of Christ in all the glorious and messy, ordinary and startling details of our lives. The joys and sorrows of our life are the dying and rising of Christ going on in us, drawing us always closer to God and one another in love. Nothing in our life is useless.

In liturgy and in our prayers of praise, all this good and loving work of God is present in Christ through the power of his Spirit. Our service of praise rises out of our wonder and admiration for the divine goodness at work in our lives. Liturgy and prayers of praise are our way of saying "Yes, amen!" to this work.

✧ This week include one, or parts of one, of the following psalms in your morning prayer each day: Psalms 145, 146, 147, 148, 149, and 150. Write the verse that attracts you most on a small notecard. Memorize it or put the card in your pocket so you can take it out and repeat the verse as you walk from the parking lot to work, as you go to your morning and afternoon coffee breaks and to lunch, and while you are returning to the parking lot at the end of your work day.

✧ As a part of your night prayer this week use Psalm 66. Each night make a list of that day's "tremendous . . . deeds [of God]" (verse 5) that tell you all that God does for you (verse 16). When you have finished your list, use it as a litany of praise and thanksgiving, saying each aloud followed by this refrain: "Blessed be God, / who has not rejected my prayer / or withheld steadfast love from me!" (verse 20).

✧ Memorize your favorite hymn of praise. Try to remember that, no matter what, God is good and can only love. Remember, too, that there are others around the world at this very moment who are keenly aware of God's blessings. Unite yourself with them as well as with those who are burdened and oppressed. If you are alone or in like-minded company, sing your hymn aloud.

✧ Find a quiet place in your home facing an east window. In the morning, before you do or say anything else, stand there facing the east at sunrise. Raise your hands above your head and reach toward the rising sun as a symbol of Christ Risen and with us and chant aloud three times, "O Lord, open my lips, and my mouth will proclaim your praise." Bow, and pray out loud, "Glory be to the Father, and to the Son, and to the Holy Spirit. As it was in the beginning, is now and ever shall be, world without end. Amen!" Dance if you wish. Then conclude your morning prayer in your own way.

✧ In the evening as or after the sun goes down, sit facing a window that looks west. As the natural light wanes, light a candle while remembering the presence of Christ your Light. Recall the blessings of the day. After leisurely reflecting on each blessing, say interiorly or chant aloud, "Praise and thanks to you, Risen Christ Jesus," or whatever response comes to you. When you have finished, rest quietly in the truth that the protecting, comforting presence of Christ will remain with you throughout the night.

God's Word

Alleluia!
Praise to you, Yahweh, in your sanctuary!
Praise to you in the firmament of your strength.
Praise you for your mighty deeds;
praise you for your sovereign majesty.
Praise to you, Yahweh, with the blast of the trumpet,
praise with lyre and harp.
Praise with timbrel and dance;
praise with strings and flute.

Praise to you, Yahweh, with resounding cymbals;
praise with clanging cymbals.
Let everything that has breath praise Yahweh.
Alleluia.

(Psalm 150)

Closing prayer: Praise to you gracious and loving God. In your Son, Jesus Christ, risen and with us, you fill every moment with your goodness. Through the power of his Spirit, open my heart, my mind, and my lips this day and all my days in praise of you. Alleluia!

The Word of God Is Living

Theme: Daily individual reading, listening, and respond-ing to the word of God in the Scriptures draws us more and more deeply into a personal relationship with the Word, Christ, so that finally his life becomes our life and our life be-comes his.

Opening prayer: Word of God, you are living and active in sacred Scripture. Draw me to you in that word as you drew Benedict. Help me enter through the words of Scripture into a loving relationship with you so that my life becomes wholly yours.

About Benedict

The books of the Bible were the most important holdings of the libraries in the monasteries Benedict established. No day passed without Benedict and his followers using them for the individual prayerful reading of Scripture, *lectio divina.* This constant attention to the word of God had a great effect on Benedict and his disciples.

Gregory's story about Zalla's arrival at the monastery is an icon of Benedict "the reader," whose glance and words were filled by a power beyond his own. The word of God in the Scriptures had become the word of God living and active in his life.

Zalla, a cruel Goth and an Arian heretic, had been mercilessly persecuting dedicated orthodox Christians. One farmer whom he was torturing in order to get his money finally, in desperation, told Zalla that Abbot Benedict had all of it. Not to be outmaneuvered or outwitted, Zalla mounted his horse and drove the poor farmer ahead of him to the abbey. When they arrived they found the man of God sitting alone in front of the entrance reading. "This is the Abbot Benedict I meant," he told the infuriated Goth behind him.

Imagining that this holy man could be frightened as readily as anyone else, Zalla glared at him with eyes full of hate and shouted harshly, "Get up! Do you hear? Get up and give back the money this man left with you!"

Not at all threatened, Benedict looked up calmly from his Scripture reading and took note of the poor farmer who stood before him, bound, cowering, and bleeding. As soon as Benedict's glance touched the rope that bound the farmer, "it fell miraculously to the ground. Human hands could never have unfastened it so quickly." Zalla, shocked by Benedict's power, fell at the saint's feet pleading for his prayers.

Benedict merely invited his brothers to take Zalla in and give him some refreshments. Only then did Benedict urge him to give up his heartless ways. Gregory concludes the story, "Zalla went away . . . and made no more demands on this farmer."

Gregory then reminds Peter that those who devote themselves to putting on Christ can work such miracles sometimes (*Dialogues*, pp. 63–64).

Pause: In what way has reading and praying the Scriptures affected your life?

Words of Benedict

Listen readily to holy reading, and devote yourself often to prayer. (*Rule*, 4.55–56)

Idleness is the enemy of the soul. Therefore, the brothers should have specified periods for manual labor as well as for prayerful reading.

We believe that the times for both may be arranged as follows: From Easter to the first of October, they will spend their mornings after Prime till about the fourth hour at whatever work needs to be done. From the fourth hour until the time of Sext, they will devote themselves to reading. But after Sext and their meal, they may rest on their beds in complete silence; should a brother wish to read privately, let him do so, but without disturbing the others.

From the first of October to the beginning of Lent, the brothers ought to devote themselves to reading until the end of the second hour. At this time Terce is said and they are to work at their assigned tasks until None. At the first signal for the hour of None, all put aside their work to be ready for the second signal. Then after their meal they will devote themselves to their reading or to the psalms.

During the days of Lent, they should be free in the morning to read until the third hour, after which they will work at their assigned tasks until the end of the tenth hour. During this time of Lent each one is to receive a book [of the Bible] from the library, and is to read the whole of it straight through. These books are to be distributed at the beginning of Lent.

Above all, one or two seniors must surely be deputed to make the rounds of the monastery while the brothers are reading. Their duty is to see that no brother is so apathetic as to waste time or engage in idle talk to the neglect of his reading, and so not only harm himself but also distract others.

On Sunday all are to be engaged in reading except those who have been assigned various duties. (*Rule*, 48.1–5,10–17,22)

Reading [always accompanied] the meals of the brothers. (*Rule*, 38.1)

Reflection

Attention to the word of God in *lectio divina* along with liturgy was the backbone of each day's schedule in Benedict's monasteries. No day passed without every member devoting two to four hours to *lectio*. Not even monastics have this much time to devote to *lectio*, but we all have some time. And this kind of reading remains the most basic kind of prayer, an essential component of Christian life.

The disciples of Benedict sought in their *lectio divina* a personal engagement, an intimate visit, a loving conversation, and a silent communing with Christ, with God. They were listening for the voice of the one they loved, the one with whom they longed to be fully united.

They read slowly, listening attentively to the words as they read them, then repeated them, mulling them over, until they knew them "by heart." Knowing them by heart did not just mean they memorized them, which they did, but also that their knowledge was the knowledge of love and experience. Their reading moved from repetition of words, to giving their own loving response, to quiet resting in God. *Lectio divina* is like reading a letter from a friend—something to be savored and lingered over lovingly.

✧ You may have studied the books of the Hebrew Scriptures, or Old Testament. Such study can greatly enhance prayer. Now spend some time in *lectio divina* with the Bible. The book of Exodus or the story of Ruth might be good places to begin. Take as many sessions as you need to do *lectio* from the start to the finish of the story.

Before you begin to meditate, recall that God is present within and around you and that what is being described here is somehow a symbol for what is going on in your life. As you read a passage, attend to your feelings, relationships, fears, hopes, desires, successes, and failures. Invite your imagination to work freely. Let yourself identify with the various characters. Read at a pace that is comfortable to you, but always remember that this is like a letter from a dear friend. Listen to God's words. What is God saying to you today? Enter into conversation with God. Express your feelings in personal prayer. Rest in God's presence.

✧ Read the Gospel of Mark slowly and reflectively. In what ways are you like the characters in the Gospel stories? Remember that the actions and words of Jesus in the Gospel are present to you now as they were to them. What is he doing for you? What is he saying to you?

✧ Read slowly through some of the psalms. Don't hesitate to read over and over again those parts that attract you or those parts that are repugnant to you. Memorize your favorite verses and repeat them whenever you can during the day without becoming compulsive about it. Enter into conversation with God about the parts you resist.

✧ Reread the story about Zalla in the "About Benedict" section. Recall times in your life when the word of God in Scripture has been a source of courage for you. Or recall times when you have been able to respond with love and strength beyond your power in the face of attack, or times when you have not been able to. After describing the event in detail in your imagination or in your journal, pray with the psalmist, repeating the words as long as you are moved to do so:

> God, you are my light and my salvation;
> whom shall I fear?
> You are the stronghold of my life;
> of whom shall I be afraid?
> I believe that I shall see the goodness of Yahweh
> in the land of the living!
> Wait for Yahweh;
> be strong, and let your heart take courage.
> Yes, wait for God!
>
> (Psalm 27:1,13–14)

God's Word

The word of God is living and active, sharper than any two-edged sword, piercing until it divides soul from spirit, joints from marrow; it is able to judge the thoughts and intentions of the heart. And before [God] no creature is hidden, but all are naked and laid bare to the eyes of the one to whom we must render an account. (Hebrews 4:12–13)

Closing prayer: Word of God, I thank you for your presence to me now in the words of the Scriptures. May all my words this day reflect you who are the Word Made Flesh dwelling among us. May your strength and love touch others through me.

✧ Meditation 5 ✧

Work for the Good of All

Theme: Good work is necessary for our personal and community sustenance. Our most effective work flows from an inner receptivity and rest in the creative, redeeming presence and energy of God working through us.

Opening prayer: Creating, redeeming God, give me the faith to let my whole being rest deeply in you, so that my work flows freely and generously from your creative life and glorifies you.

About Benedict

Building and maintaining a monastery, serving one another in a monastic community, receiving guests, and helping poor people required Benedict and his community to work regularly for about six hours every day. Much of their work was manual labor, quite literally, work done by hand.

Water had to be carried in from a well or stream and stored for use. There were meals to be prepared and served with no modern conveniences: two cooked dishes and whatever fresh fruit or vegetables were available from the garden. Grinding grain and baking bread were daily chores, and winemaking a seasonal one. Gardens and fields needed planting, cultivating, and harvesting, although the monks sometimes had to hire help for harvesting. However, Benedict admonished the monks not to be distressed if that is not possible, for when they work with their hands "they are really monks" (*Rule*, 48.8). Carpentry and masonry projects required quarrying stone and felling trees, transporting materials, joining boards, and fixing stones in place for new rooms and workshops.

Building up and maintaining a library meant reproducing manuscripts by hand, perhaps even preparing the sheepskin parchment. Even though copying manuscripts of the Bible could be inspiring for the monks, bending over their work for long hours, straining to avoid errors, ink blotches, and illegibility, caused hands to cramp and backs to ache.

Nursing occupied some community members. Teaching the young monks to read was another occupation essential to preparing the young monks for participation in liturgy and *lectio*. Artisans practiced their crafts, perhaps pottery making, weaving, leather working, metalworking, or woodworking, and sold their products locally. Even recycling had its place in the work schedule of the community; the clothing for which the monks had no further use was mended and regularly distributed to the poor. Necessary business away from the monastery meant that errands had to be run, some on foot, some perhaps on horseback.

In spite of the fact that a lot of work awaited them, when Benedict and his brothers jumped, rolled, or pulled themselves out of bed in the morning, they did not rush off immediately to their daily round of duties. Nor did they devote all, or even the majority, of their waking hours to work. According to the Rule, before they ever thought about getting to their work in the morning, several hours were devoted to liturgy of hours and *lectio divina*. At midmorning, noon, and midafternoon they stopped whatever they were doing to pray liturgy of hours. Rest at midday in summer, when the nights were shorter and the heat and hard work could be oppressive, was also part of their daily schedule.

Pause: How does work balance with the other important parts of your life?

Benedict's Words

First of all, every time you begin a good work, you must pray to [Christ] most earnestly to bring it to perfection. In his goodness, he has already counted us as his sons, and therefore we should never grieve him by our evil actions. With his good gifts which are in us, we must obey him at all times. (*Rule*, Prologue 4–6)

Idleness is the enemy of the soul. Therefore, the brothers should have specified periods for manual labor as well as for prayerful reading.

They must not become distressed if local conditions or their poverty should force them to do the harvesting themselves. When they live by the labor of their hands, as our fathers and the apostles did, then they are really monks. Yet, all things are to be done with moderation on account of the fainthearted. (*Rule*, 48.1,7–9)

The brothers should serve one another. Consequently, no one will be excused from kitchen service unless he is sick or engaged in some important business of the monastery; for such service increases reward and fosters love. Let those who are not strong have help so that they may serve without distress, and let everyone receive help as the size of the community or local conditions warrant. . . . Let all the rest serve one another in love.

On Saturday the brother who is completing his work will do the washing. He is to wash the towels which the brothers use to wipe their hands and feet. Both the one who is ending his service and the one who is about to begin are to wash the feet of everyone.

On Sunday immediately after Lauds, those beginning as well as those completing their week of service should make a profound bow in the oratory before all and ask for their prayers. Let the server completing his week recite this verse: Blessed are you, Lord God, who have helped me and comforted me (Dan 3:52; Ps 85[86]:17). After this verse has been said three times, he receives a blessing. Then the one beginning his service follows and says: God, come to my assistance; Lord, make haste to help me

(Ps 69[70]:2). And all repeat this verse three times. When he has received a blessing, he begins his service. (*Rule*, 35.1–9,15–18)

Reflection

Many of us seem to be obsessed with work. Ours might be one of the grim, strained, harried faces rushing to our job. Even when we are not at work, we may be working at something: our health, our family life, our relationships, even our spiritual lives. We work very hard at leisure activities, scheduling so many enjoyable things to do that we exhaust ourselves. Nevertheless, in our heart we know that there is more to life than work.

Certainly work has its place in human life. From a Christian standpoint, our work is part of the creative and redemptive work of Christ. Benedict knew that work was good for the soul and necessary for self-support and assisting poor people.

However, the Rule's perspective on work helps us see that it is only one part of the overall "work" of inner transformation, that "labor of obedience" (*Rule*, Prologue 2) that brings us back to God. In this all-encompassing transformation, work was only one of the elements of a balanced day in which enough time for prayer, meals, community life, and rest was always included.

Work comes into harmony when it flows from the inner divine source of energy. When done mindfully, animated by desire for good and an awareness of God's working in us, work tends to take its proper proportion in our life, and we are able to work with more peace, perseverance, and joy. A life of prayer nurtures every good work, whether spiritual or material.

✧ After entrusting yourself to God's presence and praying for the guidance of the Holy Spirit, make a list of all the good things your work does for you or allows in your life and your family or community. Reread your list and after each item pray, "Blessed are you, God, who have helped me and comforted me." During or after each task you do today, repeat the same prayer.

✧ Review the amount of time you spend working in a typical week by making a time chart for each day. Then converse with God about each of these questions:

✦ Does work take a disproportionate amount of my time, depriving me of necessary time for fostering my relationship with myself, others, and God?

✦ Do I have enough meaningful work in my life?

Asking for God's help, use your mind and imagination to consider ways you could live a more balanced life. If you can, conclude your prayer with thanks and praise.

✧ After praying to the Holy Spirit for guidance, reread the "Benedict's Words" section, thinking about what it might mean for your life. When you have finished, spend some time thanking God for whatever inspiration, encouragement, or challenge you experienced, or just rest silently in God's presence.

✧ As you go through your work day, notice your attitudes about the various aspects of your work. When do you feel joyful, energetic, hopeful, and happy? When do you feel bored, anxious, fearful, oppressed, or depressed? No matter what your feelings are, use these moments of awareness to repeat interiorly, "O God, come to my assistance; O Lord, make haste to help me." Keep up this practice until it becomes as natural to you as breathing.

✧ You may feel caught in a job that is a great burden to you. Reflect on ways you could find more suitable work. You may see no way out because of your financial or other obligations. Reread the Passion narrative in one of the Gospels, uniting yourself and your work with the suffering of Christ in his redeeming work. Conclude your prayer by repeating Christ's words: "'If it is possible, let this cup pass from me; yet not what I want but what you want'" (Matthew 26:39). Pray for ways in which this work you find uncomfortable can be a ministry to your customers, coworkers, the earth, and so on.

God's Word

You reap whatever you sow. So let us not grow weary in doing what is right, for we will reap at harvest time, if we do not give up. So then, whenever we have an opportunity, let us work for the good of all. (Galatians 6:7,9–10)

Closing prayer: Thank you, God, for the work that you give me to do. In all the physical, mental, emotional, and spiritual energy I expend in my labor, keep my soul always at rest in you so that my work may be yours, directed and accomplished in cooperation with your Spirit in Christ at work in me.

Watch! Pay Attention!

Theme: Watching is an essential part of every Christian life of prayer. Alert, we watch for the ways the light of Christ shines in our darkness.

Opening prayer: Help me, O God, watch for the light of Christ in and around me. And help me look forward with confidence and joy to living eternally in your light.

About Benedict

Very early every morning, in fact while it was still night, Benedict and his brothers rose and went quickly but solemnly to the oratory for vigils. During this first hour of the divine office, or liturgy of hours, they watched and prayed, most likely aware of the darkness not only around but within them. Sometimes, no doubt, the night symbolized for them an inner experience of luminous darkness in which they met a hidden presence, a night, as the psalmist says, shining as the day (adapted from Psalm 139:12). At other times they experienced the opaque darkness of sin and death. In both kinds of darkness they tried to stay alert and receptive to the light of Christ.

Sometimes, according to Gregory, Benedict stayed awake through the night or got up before the others to watch and pray. Toward the end of his life on one such occasion, his spirit was greatly enlarged and expanded in God's light. A lifetime of watching and praying had made him so receptive to the Divine Light that in this moment of special grace, he saw all things as God sees them. Gregory tells the story like this:

> At another time the deacon Servandus came to see the servant of God on one of his regular visits. He was abbot of the monastery in Campania that had been founded by the late senator Liberius, and always welcomed an opportunity to discuss with Benedict the truths of eternity, for he, too, was a man of deep spiritual understanding. In speaking of their hopes and longings they were able to taste in advance the heavenly food that was not yet fully theirs to enjoy. When it was time to retire for the night, Benedict went to his room on the second floor of the tower, leaving Servandus in the one below, which was connected with his own by a stairway. Their disciples slept in the large building facing the tower.
>
> Long before the night office began, the man of God was standing at his window, where he watched and prayed while the rest were still asleep. In the dead of night he suddenly beheld a flood of light shining down from above more brilliant than the sun, and with it every trace of darkness cleared away. Another remarkable sight followed. According to his own description, the whole world was gathered up before his eyes in what appeared to be a single ray of light. As he gazed at all this dazzling display, he saw the soul of Germanus, the bishop of Capua, being carried by angels up to heaven in a ball of fire. (*Dialogues*, pp. 70–71)

Pause: How do you watch for the Divine Light, the light of Christ in your life?

Benedict's Words

Let us get up then, at long last, for the Scriptures rouse us when they say: *It is high time for us to arise from sleep* (Rom 13:11). Let us open our eyes to the light that comes from

God, and our ears to the voice from heaven that every day calls out this charge: *If you hear his voice today, do not harden your hearts* (Ps 94[95]:8). And again: *You that have ears to hear, listen to what the Spirit says to the churches* (Rev 2:7). And what does he say? *Come and listen to me, sons; I will teach you the fear of the Lord* (Ps 33[34]:12). *Run while you have the light* of life, *that the darkness* of death *may not overtake you* (John 12:35). (*Rule*, Prologue 8–13)

Reflection

In the "dead of night" Benedict experienced "a flood of light . . . more brilliant than the sun." The dead of night may at times mean for us the soft, welcoming darkness when the day's activities are over and night blankets our world, a time to turn from our labor to the intimacy of love. Just as night is a time for human love, so it can be a time when, with our bodies and minds at rest, we become interiorly alert to the presence of the Divine Light that shines in the darkness within and around us.

The dead of night may sometimes be for us times of inner darkness when we are searching for spiritual light. Such nights may be times of temptation to hatred and sin, experiences of depression, anxiety, illness, fatigue, loss, grief, boredom, or meaninglessness. Or they may be long stretches of ordinary time when the spiritual world seems to be in a fog, hidden from our inner eye. Perhaps we have fallen asleep to its reality. When that darkness descends, the feeling that we will never see the "light of day" tends to undermine our belief in and hope for the presence of Christ's light in our darkness.

Benedict and his community found rising before dawn to pray in the dark a way to deepen their faith in and hope for the daily coming of the Divine Light, whether in luminous or opaque inner darkness. Praying in the middle of the night reminded them to watch for Christ's coming in death and for his coming at the end of time.

Whether or not we ever keep vigil physically, it is important for us to stay awake interiorly, always alert to the ways the Divine Light manifests itself. One day, of course, will be our last. Then in the night of death, our habit of watching for the light will keep us interiorly alert for the dawn of Christ's coming. And, without a doubt, one day the world as we know it will come to an end and Christ will come in glory. Watching daily for the coming of the Divine Light is a way of staying awake and alert for the coming of Christ on that day. Whether or not we, like Benedict, have a foretaste of the fullness of Divine Light in this life, we will surely see it in the next. Then we, like him, will see all things in that light.

✧ Reflect on the importance that light—sunlight, moonlight, lamplight, firelight—has in your life. Think of some instances in which you were watching and waiting for light. How did you feel while you were in the dark, waiting and watching. How did you feel when the light came? Describe your experience in your journal or let your imagination see it. Spend some time giving God thanks for the coming of the light. Give thanks for the light of Christ in your life.

✧ Some warm night when you are at peace, settle down quietly in a safe and comfortable spot outside where, insofar as it is possible, only natural light and sound surround you. Observe your breathing for a few minutes. As it slows down, turn your attention to the darkness and welcome it. To help you focus, pray interiorly, "[Your] light shines in the darkness (John 1:5)," or whatever words are given to you. Or just sit relaxed but alert to the presence in the darkness, responding in whatever way attracts you.

✧ On a day when you can spend time in the dark watching for the dawn, settle down in a quiet spot facing an east window. Light a lamp or candle as you ask God to illumine your heart with the light of Christ.

As you watch and wait for the coming of the dawn, recall the Easter candle and the celebration of Christ's Resurrection at the Easter Vigil. Pray the following parts of the "Exsultet" as often as you wish. Intersperse this prayer with long periods of silent waiting and watching.

This is the night when Christians everywhere, washed clean of sin and freed from all defilement, are restored to grace and grow together in holiness.

This is the night when Jesus Christ broke the chains of death and rose triumphant from the grave.

The power of this holy night dispels all evil, washes guilt away, restores lost innocence, and brings mourners joy.

Night truly blessed when heaven is wedded to earth and [we are] reconciled with God!

Therefore, heavenly Father, in the joy of this night, receive our evening sacrifice of praise, your Church's solemn offering.

Accept this Easter candle. May it always dispel the darkness of this night! May the Morning Star which never sets find this flame still burning: Christ, that Morning Star, who came back from the dead, and shed his peaceful light on all mankind, your Son who lives and reigns for ever and ever. Amen.

(*The Roman Missal*, pp. 178–181)

When dawn breaks, stand and give thanks for the light of Christ that illumines the world and your heart.

✧ Describe in your journal or bring to mind the most annoying or gripping darkness that lurks around the edges or seems to take over your soul at this point in your life—some fear, anger, depression, or hatred—whatever it is. Describe the particular persons or event involved and your feelings. Then sit quietly and let it be. Conclude your prayer by imaging yourself opening your soul to the light of Christ, if you can. Pray for the light of Christ to shine within, drive away fear, and heal you.

✧ Imagine how you would like to experience Christ meeting you when you die and at the end of time. Would you like Christ to meet you in this way in your daily life now? If so, with that image in mind, pray, "Come, Christ Jesus."

God's Word

Pay attention, and watch! Be alert! You cannot know when your time will come. It is like people taking a journey away from home. They tell their helpers which duties need to be performed, and they place a guard at the gate. Watch. Listen. You don't know when the owners of the home will come back. Maybe early in the morning, or at sunset, or in the middle of the night. You better not let them discover you sleeping on the job. So, be ready. Pay attention. (Adapted from Mark 13:33–37)

Closing prayer: O God, thank you for helping me stay awake and watch for your coming in Christ. Thank you for the grace to welcome him with the eyes of faith today. In the night of death and at the end of time may the dawn of his light lead me into eternal day.

✧ **Meditation 7** ✧

The Noble Weapon
of Obedience

Theme: Growing in union with Christ means listening intently for the voice of God and desiring to live in harmony with the Divine Will.

Opening prayer: Christ Jesus, I want to live in love with you. Teach me to listen for your voice, and help me respond cheerfully without delay so that the life-giving will of God may be done in me.

About Benedict

The power of free and unhesitating obedience is illustrated by Gregory in a story about Abbot Benedict and his young disciples Placid and Maurus.

Once while blessed Benedict was in his room, one of his monks, the boy Placid, went down to get some water. In letting the bucket fill too rapidly, he lost his balance and was pulled into the lake, where the current quickly seized him and carried him about a stone's throw from the shore. Though inside the monastery at the time, the man of God was instantly aware of what had happened and called out to Maurus: "Hurry, Brother Maurus! The boy who just went down for water has fallen into the lake, and the current is carrying him away."

What followed was remarkable indeed, and unheard of since the time of Peter the apostle. Maurus asked for the blessing and on receiving it hurried out to fulfill his abbot's command. He kept on running even over the water till he reached the place where Placid was drifting along helplessly. Pulling him up by the hair, Maurus rushed back to shore, still under the impression that he was on dry land. It was only when he set foot on the ground that he came to himself and looking back realized that he had been running on the surface of the water. Overcome with fear and amazement at a deed he would never have thought possible, he returned to his abbot and told him what had taken place.

The holy man would not take any personal credit for the deed but attributed it to the obedience of his disciple. Maurus on the contrary claimed that it was due entirely to his abbot's command. He could not have been responsible for the miracle himself, he said, since he had not even known he was performing it. While they were carrying on this friendly contest of humility, the question was settled by the boy who had been rescued. "When I was being drawn out of the water," he told them, "I saw the abbot's cloak over my head; he is the one I thought was bringing me to shore." (*Dialogues*, pp. 20–22)

Pause: In what ways do I listen for and respond to God's voice?

Benedict's Words

Listen carefully . . . to the master's instructions, and attend to them with the ear of your heart. This is advice from a father who loves you; welcome it, and faithfully put it into practice. The labor of obedience will bring you back to him from whom you had drifted through the sloth of disobedience. This message of mine is for you, then, if you are ready to give up your own will, once and for all, and armed with the strong and noble weapons of obedience to do battle for the true King, Christ the Lord. (*Rule*, Prologue 1–3)

The first step of humility is unhesitating obedience, which comes naturally to those who cherish Christ above all. . . . The Lord says of [these]: *No sooner did [they] hear than [they] obeyed me* (Ps 17[18]:45); again, he tells teachers: *Whoever listens to you, listens to me* (Luke 10:16). Such people as these immediately put aside their own concerns, abandon their own will, and lay down whatever they have in hand, leaving it unfinished. With the ready step of obedience, they follow the voice of authority in their actions. Almost at the same moment, then, as the master gives the instruction the disciple quickly puts it into practice in the fear of God; and both actions together are swiftly completed as one.

This very obedience, however, will be acceptable to God and agreeable to [others] only if compliance with what is commanded is not cringing or sluggish or half-hearted, but free from any grumbling or any reaction of unwillingness." (*Rule*, 5:1–2,5–9,14)

Reflection

Christian obedience is not just a matter of carrying out the orders of legitimate authority for the sake of accomplishing a task or keeping good order. Christian obedience comes from a response of love to God who loves us. It means giving our free inner assent to the Divine Will.

God's will comes from within our heart and through others with whom we live and work—all of them, not only those who hold particular positions of authority. God's will is being revealed to us in many ways in our daily life: through nature; through our thoughts, images, affections, desires, and aspirations; and through the community—the voices, actions, and needs of those with whom we share our life and world.

Christian formation is a process of learning to listen carefully with the ear of our heart and to respond to the life-giving voice of God. This requires distinguishing that voice from things that only appear to be good. Benedict himself had to cultivate spiritual attentiveness to God's voice in prayer. Listening "with the ear of our heart" to the voice of God within us and around us is prayer. With God's help, we can hear and respond to God's will and thus become more united to Christ. Then Christ's love can reach others through us.

✧ Reread the Placid and Maurus story in the "About Benedict" section. Think about a time in your life when an unhesitating, positive response to a person or situation resulted in renewed life for someone. Even if you were not conscious of this event as a response to Christ's voice at the time, let the incident be present in memory and imagination now. Respond to Christ's presence and voice in whatever way you feel drawn.

✧ Call to mind any current struggle or confusion you are having about knowing what God's will for you is. Mull over and converse with Christ Jesus about these and other unanswered questions that you have:

✦ Would doing just what others want me to do be your will?
✦ Would not doing what others want me to do be your will?
✦ Would doing what I feel drawn to be your will?
✦ Would undertaking this enterprise and failing mean that I did not do your will?
✦ Will you be with me in whatever I choose to do to the best of my ability?

Conclude your prayer by accepting any confusion you feel, repeating this psalm verse as often as it gives you strength: "I am a pilgrim on earth. / Show me your commands." (Psalm 119:19)

✧ Slowly reread the "Benedict's Words" section. Stop at whatever touches your heart with love and joy or with resistance and sadness. Write about what it is in you that gives rise to these feelings. Talk to the Risen Christ, who is lovingly listening to you, and tell him exactly how you feel.

✧ Recall some recent incidents when you have grumbled about something clearly required of you. Grumbling does not mean recognizing and groaning about or admitting the difficulty of something to oneself or another, but rather a kind of inner resistance, an unwillingness, a grudging response. Choose one of these incidents. Place yourself in the presence of Christ and imagine his desiring your response because of his personal love for you. Relive the incident, responding now as one who cherishes Christ above all. Ask his forgiveness for your failure to recognize his love.

✧ Pray frequently today this phrase from the Lord's Prayer: Thy kingdom come, thy will be done. Let it continue to pray itself in you while you are engaged in things that allow for your awareness at several levels.

God's Word

Wonderful are your sayings;
therefore I observe them.
The revelation of your words sheds light,
giving understanding to the simple.
I open my mouth and sigh
in my yearning for your commands.
Turn to me in pity
as you turn to those who love your name.
Free my footsteps according to your promise
and let no evil rule over me.
Redeem me from oppression
that I may keep your precepts.
Let your face shine upon your servant,
and teach me your statutes.
My eyes shed streams of tears
because your law has not been kept.
(Psalm 119:129–136)

Closing prayer: Thank you, Christ Jesus, for increasing my desire to live in union with you. Help me in the joys and struggles of this day to listen for your voice, and to respond with inner promptness and good cheer.

Be Still!
And Know That I Am God

Theme: In silence we learn to hear the voice of Christ within and around us.

Opening prayer: O God, as I turn aside from the noise of the world around me to enter the inner silence, quiet also the clamoring voices of my heart so that I can hear the voice of your son, Jesus Christ.

About Benedict

Benedict's Rule structured the day-to-day atmosphere of the monastery so that it nurtured the monks' inner life. Loud talk, vulgarity, gossip, and raucous laughter seldom disturbed the quiet. Whether copying manuscripts, clearing land, constructing buildings, planting, cultivating, or harvesting crops, cleaning, sewing, cooking, or caring for their elderly, sick, or young brothers, the monks ordinarily stayed calmly intent on their work and prayer.

In spite of occasional outbursts or more subtle infractions of the rules about when, how, and to whom to speak, a quiet peace and serenity permeated the monastery. At times during the day, monks quietly conferred with one another about their work, gently encouraging one another in difficulty and fatigue, or softly murmuring phrases from Scripture, but those words seemed to flow out of and back into the silence.

The monks ate their meals in silence, too: "No whispering, no speaking—only the reader's voice [could] be heard there" as he read the word of God from the Scriptures or an instructive commentary (*Rule*, 38.5).

> The brothers . . . by turn [served] one another's needs as they [ate and drank], so that no one need[ed to] ask for anything. If, however, anything [was] required, it [was] requested by an audible signal of some kind rather than by speech. No one [was to] presume to ask a question about the reading or about anything else, *lest occasion be given* [to the devil] (Eph 4:27; 1 Tim 5:14). The superior, however, [sometimes said] a few words of instruction. (*Rule*, 38.6–9)

The chanting of the divine office in choir was punctuated by periods of silence for inner prayer between the psalms and after the readings. Afterward "all [left] in complete silence and with reverence for God, so that a brother who [wished] to pray alone [would] not be disturbed by the insensitivity of another" (*Rule*, 52.2–3).

After compline, the night prayer recited or chanted together by heart, absolute silence reigned. No one was permitted to speak at night "except on occasions when guests require[d] attention or the abbot wishe[d] to give someone a command, but even [that was] done with the utmost seriousness and proper restraint" (*Rule*, 42.10–11). The monks' silence allowed them to hear God's voice, whether in the whisper of the wind or in the hearty proclamation of the Good News.

Pause: Reflect on the opportunities you take for silence in your life and on what happens within you during those times.

Benedict's Words

Let us follow the Prophet's counsel: *I said, I have resolved to keep watch over my ways that I may never sin with my tongue. I was silent and was humbled, and I refrained even from good words* (Ps 38[39]:2–3). Here the Prophet indicates that there are times when good words are to be left unsaid out of esteem for silence. . . . Indeed, so important is silence that permission to speak should seldom be granted even to mature disciples, no matter how good or holy or constructive their talk, because it is written: *In a flood of words you will not avoid sin* (Prov 10:19); and elsewhere, *The tongue holds the key to life and death* (Prov 18:21). Speaking and teaching are the master's task; the disciple is to be silent and listen. (*Rule*, 6.1–6)

Reflection

When he wrote his Rule, Benedict included silence as one of the key aspects of monastic life and spirituality. The Rule aims to cultivate that deep inner silence that can be conveyed with or without words. This inner silence cannot be found without some restraint of speech and some times of exterior silence. Too much noise and too many words can keep us from hearing the word of God. Benedict also knew that when speech is unrestrained, the sins of gossip, boastfulness, sarcasm, or making destructive comments are hard to avoid.

Monks spoke with one another. Silence and speech do not necessarily contradict one another. Words can be filled with the deep inner peace that comes from silence. And both silence and speech can be filled with the din of fears, hatred, or desires. External silence filled with destructive thoughts and feelings is just as noisy as negative speech.

Nevertheless, in silence we can listen with the ear of our heart to God's voice. When we still our voices, we tend to notice things that we may otherwise miss: the way a ray of sunlight falls on a vase or highlights the grain of wood in a table, or an all but hidden look of pain behind the smile of a friend. God speaks to us in all these ways. We also need a certain amount of quiet in order to be in touch with what is going on inside us so we can bring ourselves honestly, as we are, to our Scripture prayer.

External silence gives us the opportunity to become aware of inner noise. Some simple practice can help us rest in God beyond words, concepts, and feelings. This helps us to be more in touch with the deeper meaning of words in the rest of our life. All spiritualities recognize the essential role that silence plays in relating to the Divine, balancing our priorities, and developing inner peace. Cultivating silence nurtures our whole growth in Christ.

✧ Centering prayer, a form of meditation rooted in ancient tradition, is simple and can be useful in deepening our inner silence.

Before you begin, sit in a chair or on a cushion in a way that keeps you relaxed but alert, with your back flexibly straight, and your hands resting on your knees or in your lap. If you only have a specific period of time available, set a timer to go off or place your watch or clock in a position where you can check it without moving. Breathe deeply and, if your body feels cramped, do some gentle stretching. Close your eyes or keep them downcast and softly focused on one spot on the floor or wall that is not distracting. Then begin, using the following four steps.

✦ Remember the presence of God's Holy Spirit dwelling within you.

✦ Choose a short word like God, Jesus, love, or peace. Introduce it gently in your imagination as a sign of your faith in God's presence and work in you through and in the Spirit of the Risen Christ. Repeat the word inwardly. You need not say the word aloud or even move your lips or tongue.

✦ When you notice yourself being attracted to some thought or feeling—and you inevitably will—gently repeat your word as a sign of your intention to simply rest in God's presence and action, letting the thought float down the stream of your consciousness. The use of the word may sometimes reduce the flow of thoughts in your mind; sometimes it does not. There is no need to empty your mind. The point is, rather, to be detached from the thoughts

and feelings. Keep the same word during the entire prayer
period.

✦ When your time for centering prayer is over, conclude with
the Lord's Prayer or some other prayer. Stretch and move
gently. Spend a little time planning for the day, knowing
that God is with you in the Spirit of Christ.

If you are attracted to this kind of prayer, remember that
it can be done anytime, anyplace, but you might get the most
benefit from it using a steady pattern of twenty-minute sessions in a quiet place.

✧ Tomorrow when you get up, don't turn on the radio,
TV, or music. When you shower, dress, and have breakfast, do
so as quietly and gently as you can. Set aside a few minutes
before you leave for or begin your day's work to note in your
journal what you noticed around and within yourself. What
sights and sounds did you become aware of? What thoughts
and feelings were arising within you? Thank God for this
awareness and entrusting of everything to the divine goodness.

✧ Choose a short Scripture phrase that speaks to you, for
instance:

For God alone my soul waits.
My help comes from God.

(Psalm 62:1)

Repeat the phrase during any silent time you have, like when
you are driving. When you feel more calm, let go of the phrase
and let your soul wait on God. Attend to what is going on
around you, taking it in whether it is the driver in front of you
or the remembrance of your wife, a friend, your husband, or
your child, and remember that person's needs and desires or
love for you. Then, remembering God, quietly and slowly repeat your Scripture phrase with that in mind.

✧ Make it a point to be silent and listen to others before
you speak. At the end of the day, reflect on what difference, if
any, this approach to others had. What responses did it bring

up in you? Did you notice any way it evoked responses from your friends or associates that were different from the usual ones?

✧ Reread the "About Benedict" section. Think about a typical day in your life, perhaps the day just past or the one coming up. If silence is a value for you, in what ways could you incorporate more of it in a typical day?

God's Word

"Be still! and know that I am God,
exalted among the nations, exalted upon the earth."
(Psalm 46:10)

Closing prayer: Gracious and loving God, you have spoken to me beyond word and sound in the silence of your Word, Jesus Christ. May the silence of that Word fill all my silences and speech this day, communicating your love and goodness.

✧ Meditation 9 ✧

Born in Human Likeness

Theme: Growth in prayer brings us to a loving acceptance of ourselves as we are, blessed with many gifts, but limited and sinful. Most importantly it brings us to a joy-filled worship of God.

Opening prayer: Majestic and loving Creator, lead me during this time of prayer to a deeper knowledge, love, and acceptance of myself and to a more joyful worship of your goodness in myself, in others, and in you.

About Benedict

While talking about Benedict's gift of prophecy in the *Dialogues,* Gregory tells two stories that point out the importance of humility as a noninflated self-acceptance that does not depend on any kind of role, status, recognition, or deference to support an illusion of superiority.

One time a cleric from a town near Monte Cassino was suffering the torments of an evil spirit. Constantius, his bishop, sent him to the shrines of various martyrs for help. Finally, the poor man came to Benedict, who, "with fervent prayers to Christ" (*Dialogues,* p. 38) was able to free him. Before he sent him home, he told him never to be ordained a deacon or a priest or he would again be tormented.

The cleric left completely cured, and as long as his previous torments were still fresh in his mind he did exactly as the man of God had ordered. Then, with the passing of years, all his seniors in the clerical state died, and he had to watch newly ordained young men moving ahead of him in rank. Finally he pretended to have forgotten about the saint's warning and, disregarding it, presented himself for ordination. Instantly he was seized by the devil and tormented mercilessly until he died. (*Dialogues*, p. 39)

On another occasion Benedict reprimands one of the brothers for his arrogant spirit.

Once when the saintly abbot was taking his evening meal, a young monk whose father was a high-ranking official happened to be holding the lamp for him. As he stood at the abbot's table the spirit of pride began to stir in his heart. "Who is this," he thought to himself, "that I should have to stand here holding the lamp for him while he is eating? Who am I to be serving him?"

Turning to him at once, Benedict gave the monk a sharp reprimand. "Brother," he said, "sign your heart with the sign of the Cross. What are you saying? Sign your heart!" Then calling the others together, he had one of them take the lamp instead, and told the murmurer to sit down by himself and be quiet. Later, when asked what he had done wrong, the monk explained how he had given in to the spirit of pride and silently murmured against the man of God. (*Dialogues*, pp. 46–47)

Pause: Have there been times in your life when striving after a role or recognition of your status or importance has obscured your relationship with God and others?

Benedict's Words

In accord with previous monastic tradition, in chapter 7 of the *Rule*, Benedict describes growth in the life of prayer in terms of the ladder of humility, saying that "we descend by exaltation and ascend by humility" (7.7). The ladder has twelve rungs that describe the kind of transformation that, with our cooperation and effort, a life of prayer effects in us. Through the work of the Holy Spirit in us, the ladder finally brings us to that *"perfect love* of God which *casts out fear"* (*Rule*, 7.67 quoting 1 John 4:18). The rungs of the ladder of humility can be paraphrased in this way:

1. Continual reverent mindfulness of God and watchfulness over our behavior and inner thoughts

2. Desire to live in harmony with God's will

3. Willingness to respond to others' legitimate desires and commands out of love for God

4. Quiet acceptance of necessary suffering in life without finally succumbing in our struggles with anger, depression, and the desire to run away

5. Straightforward revelation of our inner thoughts, good and bad, to a mature and trusted other

6. Contentment with shabby treatment by others

7. Sincere and peaceful acknowledgment in our heart that we are no better and could very well be worse than others

8. Ability to live in community without the compulsion to establish or make a point of our unique identity by acting contrary to others

9. Capacity to refrain from speaking on every topic and in every situation

10. Avoidance of silly, sarcastic, and demeaning laughter

11. Simple, gentle, authentic self-presentation

12. Quiet, nonostentacious bodily demeanor
    The sixth and seventh steps of humility are turning points in the life of prayer. They describe a radical change in the way we experience ourselves.

> The sixth step of humility is that a [monastic] is content with the lowest and most menial treatment, and regards himself as a poor and worthless [worker] in whatever task he is given, saying to himself with the Prophet: *I am*

insignificant and ignorant, no better than a beast before you, yet I am with you always (Ps 72[73]:22–23).

The seventh step of humility is that a man not only admits with his tongue but is also convinced in his heart that he is inferior to all and of less value, humbling himself and saying with the Prophet: *I am truly a worm, not [human], scorned by [others] and despised by the people* (Ps 21[22]:7). *I was exalted, then I was humbled and overwhelmed with confusion* (Ps 87[88]:16). And again, *It is a blessing that you have humbled me so that I can learn your commandments* (Ps 118[119]:71,73). (*Rule*, 7.49–54)

Reflection

A life of prayer draws us more deeply into God's love for us. When the greatness of God and our own nothingness without the divine love become the ground on which we rest, our desperate need for a separate self-importance vanishes. We are free from the tendency either to self-inflation or self-deprecation.

In prayer we come to experience that we are secure in God's love. This gradually opens us to see, admit, and rejoice in our total dependence on God and to be content with our own unique gifts. As that happens, we are able to let go of any need either to boast about or to belittle ourselves, whether outwardly to others or interiorly to ourselves.

The more secure we become in God's unique love for us, the more free we become not to be unduly upset by poor treatment from others. Our worth depends less and less on external recognition.

When we believe we are loved by God, we can relax as with a friend and let all aspects of ourselves be known. We can admit our mistakes and sins because we know we are accepted and acceptable. In true humility, we no longer need to think of ourselves as better than others, nor to pity ourselves because we are worse than others. What we know more surely is that we are nothing without God. We do not create our own goodness, nor do we earn God's love by our efforts. We can only receive that goodness and love, and let that be the energy that motivates our good actions. Embracing this truth is what humility is all about.

✧ Recall the times and places in your life when you have been and are amazed by God's greatness: particular places in nature, times spent in the loving or creative presence of another person, or events like a birth or death. Write a description of the place, person, or event in some detail with all the feelings that accompanied it. Let yourself be drawn into whatever responses are evoked now. Respond to God, the source of all good.

✧ Reread the "About Benedict" section. Recall times in your life when, like the beleaguered cleric, you set out to achieve some goal that did not suit your personality or gifts, to be someone you are not. Spend some time reflecting and writing about one of these. What motivated you? What physical, psychological, emotional, and spiritual effects did your misguided efforts have in your life? What inner and outer events changed your course? How did you feel then? When you have completed your reflection, turn to God and give thanks for your uniqueness, if you can. If not, express whatever your honest responses are.

✧ Reread the "About Benedict" section with a focus on the proud young monk. Then reflect on some recent occasion when you have compared yourself to others and judged yourself either better or worse. What feelings accompanied your judgment? Is there some insecurity in you that evoked this judgment and these feelings? Accepting that insecurity as compassionately as you can, put your trust in the divine mercy. Addressing God in whatever way suits you, for instance, God, Jesus, Loving Spirit, Gracious Source of Life, Friend, Mother, Father, spend some time telling God simply and honestly what happened and asking for whatever it is you think you need.

Then read the following words from Jeremiah slowly a number of times, listening to them as God's response to you:

"I have loved you with an everlasting love; therefore I have continued my faithfulness to you" (31:3).

✧ Read the account of Christ's Passion and death from one of the Gospels. Reflect on how despised Christ was by others.

Then reread the sixth and seventh steps of humility in the "Benedict's Words" section. Remember that it was God's love for Christ that brought him through the humiliation of his death into his risen life. Now recall some recent or past undeserved rebuffs by others that you have experienced, or call to mind some undertaking in which you felt yourself a failure. Unite your will to Christ's, letting go of your desire for approval or success, repeating with Christ, "'Into your hands I commend my spirit'" (Luke 23:46).

God's Word

Let the same mind be in you that was in Christ Jesus,
who, though he was in the form of God,
did not regard equality with God
as something to be exploited,
but emptied himself,
taking the form of a slave,
being born in human likeness.
And being found in human form,
he humbled himself
and became obedient to the point of death—
even death on a cross.
Therefore God also highly exalted him
and gave him the name
that is above every name,
so that at the name of Jesus
every knee should bend,
in heaven and on earth and under the earth,
and every tongue should confess
that Jesus Christ is Lord,
to the glory of God the Father.

(Philippians 2:5–11)

Closing prayer: Christ Jesus, you amaze me because you who alone are worthy of all glory did not consider being divine something to cling to, but wanted to be human like us. Help me to accept, love, and rejoice in my humanity just as it is, without pretentiousness or shame, trusting in your love and mercy. Help me lose myself in wonder at your goodness and love.

✧ Meditation 10 ✧

Abide in My Love

Theme: A life of communion with God in prayer depends on stability of heart, an inner rootedness and tranquillity that keep us steadfast in joys and trials. God's stability, God's faithfulness, makes our stability possible.

Opening prayer: Faithful God, you are our rock of certainty, always with us in Christ. Open me to your steadfast loving presence during this time of prayer, and teach me how to remain with you now and always.

About Benedict

In Book III of the *Dialogues,* Gregory recounts several miraculous events associated with a hermit named Martin who lived in a cave not too far from Benedict's monastery. Once settled there, Martin never left his wilderness retreat on the steep, wooded mountainside. Gregory concludes his stories about Martin's holiness and influence on the local people who sought him out by noting the important way Benedict's words affected the hermit's stability.

When Martin first came to this mountain, before he had shut himself up in the cave, he fastened an iron chain to his foot and fixed the other end of it into a rock, thus removing all possibility of going any farther than the length of chain would allow.

When the saintly Benedict, of whom I spoke previously, heard of this, he sent one of his disciples to Martin with this message: "If you are a servant of God you ought to be bound by the chain which is Christ and not by a chain of iron." Obedient to this advice, Martin immediately loosed the chain, but never again set foot beyond the space to which it had confined him. Having now cast the chain aside, he kept himself within the narrow circle as strictly as before. (*Dialogues,* Book III, p. 144)

Benedict's words "never failed to take effect," Gregory asserts, "because his heart was fixed in God" (*Dialogues,* p. 52). Inner stability, having his heart fixed in God, made it possible for Benedict to stay in his own hermitage at Subiaco when "almost overcome in the struggle, he was on the point of abandoning the lonely wilderness" (*Dialogues,* p. 7). Inner stability also made it possible for him to move after the monks of Vicovaro tried to poison him. Benedict realized the impossibility of his doing anything for them as their abbot, as Gregory notes in the following words:

Still calm and undisturbed, [Benedict] rose at once and after gathering the community together addressed them. "May almighty God have mercy on you," he said. "Why did you conspire to do this? Did I not tell you at the outset that my way of life would never harmonize with yours? Go and find yourselves an abbot to your liking. It is impossible for me to stay here any longer." Then he went back to the wilderness he loved, to live alone with himself in the presence of his heavenly Father. (*Dialogues,* p. 11)

Pause: Take some time to reflect on what gives you inner stability in all the changing moods and seasons of life.

Benedict's Words

When we have used [the tools of the spiritual craft] without ceasing day and night and have returned them on judgment day, our wages will be the reward the Lord has promised: *What the eye has not seen nor the ear heard, God has prepared for those who love him* (1 Cor 2:9).

The workshop where we are to toil faithfully at all these tasks is the enclosure of the monastery and stability in the community. (*Rule*, 4.76–78)

Scripture has it: *Anyone who perseveres to the end will be saved* (Matt 10:22), and again, *Be brave of heart and rely on the Lord* (Ps 26[27]:14). Another passage shows how the faithful must endure everything, even contradiction, for the Lord's sake, saying in the person of those who suffer, *For your sake we are put to death continually; we are regarded as sheep marked for slaughter* (Rom 8:36; Ps 43[44]:22). They are so confident in their expectation of reward from God that they continue joyfully and say, *But in all this we overcome because of him who so greatly loved us* (Rom 8:37). (*Rule*, 7.36–39)

Reflection

For Benedictine monastics, stability ordinarily means remaining in the same community for life, staying in relationship with the same people, and growing in love together through good times and bad. The monastery of a Benedictine's profession is the place where she or he belongs. It remains home. Stability of place and of community relationships celebrates and fosters inner stability in God.

Rootedness in a place and fidelity in relationships are important aspects of every Christian's life. The particular people to whom we are committed and the particular place we call home are for us meeting places with God in Christ. Growing in relationships with others who share the same home requires standing firm and learning to remain calm and undisturbed. It means being willing to share patiently in Christ's suffering so we may also share in his glory. This is possible only because of God's fidelity to us.

Sometimes inner stability requires that we make external changes. When, as in the life of Benedict, remaining in the same place or relationship is destructive, fidelity to God calls us to move on. Knowing when to go or when to stay is not always easy, but God will not abandon us in our suffering.

In the midst of the inevitable trials and temptations, great strength can be found by turning to God within, who, in Christ, is suffering and dying in us. God assures us of the Divine Presence and action through the covenant established with us during the Exodus from Egypt and in the Risen Christ who invites us: "'Abide in me as I abide in you'" (John 15:4). This divine fidelity in Christ is the source of our inner stability. The support we find in solid relationships and in a sense of home manifests this divine fidelity.

✧ Sit in a chair with your back straight but not rigid, head upright with chin slightly tucked in, feet firmly on the floor or ground, and hands resting quietly in your lap or palms down on your knees. Or, if you are accustomed to doing so, sit cross-legged on the floor or ground with your back and head erect. Close your eyes, or partially close them and focus on a single area of the floor. Attend quietly to your breathing for five or ten minutes. Just observe it, don't control it. There is no need to rush or slow down. Let the sounds around you and the way your body feels enter into your consciousness. Identify the various sensations and let them go. When you are relaxed, repeat slowly and interiorly, "God, you alone are my rock, my strength, my fortress. I stand firm" (adapted from Psalm 62:1), or Christ's words, "'Abide in me as I abide in you'" (John 15:4).

✧ Reread the "About Benedict" section, keeping in mind any current struggles to stay in a place, job, or relationship. Calmly express your belief that Christ is giving you the inner stability you need. Then let whatever feelings are connected with this challenge come into your consciousness, with no intention to solve any problem or make any resolution. Just let them come, and let them go. Again take up the brief sentence or phrase that expresses your faith in Christ's presence within you giving you inner stability. Conclude with some brief expression of gratitude either in words or in gestures, such as a deep bow or lifting up your hands and arms.

✧ Go in your imagination to the attic or basement of your soul, and open the trunk full of photos and snapshots of people and places that is there. Let yourself shuffle through them in no particular order. Be alert to those that stir up a

striking sense of being at home. As you find each one, stop and enjoy it. Draw, paint, color, or describe your impressions of that person or place and whatever it is or was about it, her, or him that makes you feel so at home with yourself. Conclude your prayer by recalling that God in Christ was and is present as the firm foundation of your life in those gifts of person or place.

✧ Take some time to get in touch with whatever kind of suffering you are undergoing. Let yourself feel the weight of it, the pain of it. Now reread the "Benedict's Words" section. Stop at whatever phrase gives you courage or strength. Repeat it as long as that is fruitful for you, remembering that Christ is with you in this suffering and in these words.

God's Word

"Abide in me as I abide in you. Just as the branch cannot bear fruit by itself unless it abides in the vine, neither can you unless you abide in me. I am the vine, you are the branches. Those who abide in me and I in them bear much fruit, because apart from me you can do nothing. . . . Abide in my love." (John 15:4–5,9)

Closing prayer: Faithful God, you never leave me. I am grateful for the reassurance of your presence and love in Christ, given through the Spirit in prayer today. Help me now to be alert to your abiding presence in the people and the places around me, so that I remain standing firm in life's uncertainties and suffering. Through me may you be a rock of strength for others.

✧ **Meditation 11** ✧

Various Gifts,
but the Same Spirit

Theme: Through the bond of love, Christ unites each Christian community, each Benedictine community. Though mutual respect and love, and mutual responsibility and service are hallmarks of that unity, inevitable failures in this life of love require daily forgiveness and reconciliation.

Opening prayer: Loving Spirit of God, you who are the living bond of our unity in Christ, enlighten my understanding and give new life to my spirit during this time of prayer. Help me be grateful for and committed to a life of love and service with my sisters and brothers in Christ, willing to forgive myself and them as often as we fail.

About Benedict

As cenobites, Benedict's monks lived together in a community under a rule and an abbot, united in Christ.

Ideally, mutual respect and love pervaded each monastery: "The younger monks . . . [respected] their seniors, and the seniors [loved] their juniors" (*Rule*, 63.10). When the brothers met while going about their daily routine, the younger monks would ask the seniors for a blessing. When the older monks came by, the younger ones would get up and offer them a seat. "In this way, they [did] what the words of Scripture say: *They should each try to be the first to show respect to the other* (Rom 12:10)" (*Rule*, 63.17).

Daily cooperation at prayer and work also manifested the respect and love for one another that held the community together. In addition to participating in the divine office and meals together, community members worked side by side in the fields, on building projects, while copying manuscripts, or while doing other common tasks.

The monastics had many opportunities to express their love in service. They cared for the sick and elderly among them, taught the young, received guests, and took turns serving one another: "No one [was] excused from kitchen service unless . . . sick or engaged in some important business of the monastery" (*Rule*, 35.1). They tried to foresee one another's needs and accept one another's weaknesses.

Responsible participation in decision making was another way the monks manifested their love for one another. On any given day the abbot might call the entire community together to give him counsel regarding major decisions. Even the youngest members had the privilege and responsibility of coming to these consultations as equals, because "the Lord often reveals what is better to the younger" (*Rule*, 3.3). During these meetings all were expected "to express their opinions with all humility, and not presume to defend their own views obstinately. The decision [was] rather the abbot's to make, so that when he [had] determined what [was] more prudent, all [might] obey" (*Rule*, 3.4–5). What was best for the community held paramount importance.

A variety of personalities joined Benedict's monastery. Some members were freeborn, others had been slaves, some were recent converts from the barbarian tribes that had invaded Italy, and others came from well-established Roman families. Some were "undisciplined and restless," some "obedient and docile and patient," others "negligent and disdainful" (*Rule*, 2.25). In the closeness of their life together, they no doubt sometimes got one another's nerves and were not cooperative, loving, respectful, or willing to serve.

Because of inevitable disagreements and minor rebellions in community life, Benedict built into his Rule processes for reconciliation, ways of making satisfaction for failures, seeking forgiveness, and being brought back into full community participation. One of the regular ways for repairing broken bonds and restoring harmony was the twice daily recitation of the Lord's Prayer by the abbot. This was done during the divine office and according to Benedict's own directions:

> Assuredly, the celebration of Lauds and Vespers must never pass by without the superior's reciting the entire Lord's Prayer at the end for all to hear, because thorns of contention are likely to spring up. Thus warned by the pledge they make to one another in the very words of this prayer: *Forgive us as we forgive* (Matt 6:12), they may cleanse themselves of this kind of vice. (*Rule,* 13.12–13)

Pause: Reflect on the ways in which you express love, respect, cooperation, service, and responsibility in one of the communities to which you belong.

Words of Benedict

> Just as there is a wicked zeal of bitterness which separates from God and leads to hell, so there is a good zeal which separates from evil and leads to God and everlasting life. This, then, is the good zeal which [monastics] must foster with fervent love: *They should each try to be the first to show respect to the other* (Rom 12:10), supporting with the greatest patience one another's weaknesses of body or behavior, and earnestly competing in obedience to one another. No one is to pursue what he judges better for himself, but instead, what he judges better for someone else. To [one another] they show the pure love of brothers; to God, loving fear; to their abbot, unfeigned and humble love. Let them prefer nothing whatever to Christ, and may he bring us all together to everlasting life. (*Rule,* 72)

Reflection

The Spirit within and among us unites us with Christ and so with all our sisters and brothers in him, no matter what our differences are. A life of prayer, that is, a life of relationship with Christ in the Spirit, cannot be separated from a life of responsible relationships with others. Prayer strengthens and is strengthened by the bonds of community.

Christian community may involve sharing responsibility with and living together in a family or community group. It may mean accepting an office or service position in our local parishes, schools, or other organizations. Community may mean taking whatever responsibility we can for our life together on the local, national, and global levels. Fundamentally, Christian community requires working together and serving one another's needs.

The foundation of *Christian* community is an attitude of mutual respect and love for our brothers and sisters as equals loved by God. God's love at work in us makes it possible for us to be faithful and steadfast in giving and receiving such respect and love. Love abides at the heart of community life. It is the rock on which community is built.

✧ We all live in several communities. Ponder a Christian community that is primary for you, perhaps your family, your parish, or a prayer or study group. In spirit invite each member of your community into your presence. As they come one by one, consider all of the particular gifts of love, respect, cooperation, and service that you have received from that person. After each encounter give thanks to God for these particular manifestations of divine love.

✧ Begin your prayer time in the way described above. This time, as each person comes into your presence, recall the particular gifts of love, respect, cooperation, and service the Spirit has made it possible for you to give that person. Again, after each encounter, give thanks to God for the ability to manifest love in that particular way.

✧ Let yourself become aware of any ways you have offended any member of your community, or they you. Recall the incidents, feel the pain and anger; don't gloss over it. As humbly and sincerely as you can, seek God's mercy and let go of the hurt and anger, addressing the person by name, saying: "I forgive you for _____." If you have hurt someone, pray for the light and strength to ask for forgiveness in a way that will be healing for both of you. Conclude by praying the Lord's Prayer. Pray it aloud if you are alone.

✧ Reread the "About Benedict" section. Asking God for light and courage, prayerfully open your mind and heart to any inspiration to change your attitudes about and approaches to your own community life.

✧ Pray the Lord's Prayer out loud very slowly each morning and evening, recalling specific incidents requiring your forgiveness or your need for forgiveness from others.

God's Word

Now there are varieties of gifts, but the same Spirit; and there are varieties of services, but the same Lord; and there are varieties of activities, but it is the same God who activates all of them in everyone.

Now you are the body of Christ and individually members of it.

If I speak in the tongues of mortals and of angels, but do not have love, I am a noisy gong or a clanging cymbal.

Love is patient; love is kind; love is not envious or boastful or arrogant or rude. . . . It bears all things, believes all things, hopes all things, endures all things. (1 Corinthians 12:4–6,27; 13:1–8)

Closing prayer: Spirit of love, thank you for opening my mind and heart to your love at work in my community life. Keep me attentive and responsive to your respectful, accepting, forgiving love as I talk to, work with, and serve my sisters and brothers in all the varied ways my life presents to me this day.

✧ Meditation 12 ✧

Faithful Stewards

Theme: Care for material goods, trust in God for all that we need, and willingness to share what we have with others are basic attitudes in a loving relationship with God.

Opening prayer: Gracious God, you create the world and all its fullness. Stir up the Spirit of Christ in me so that I may grow in respect for the material goods around me, trust you for all that I need, and grow in my desire to be generous with others.

About Benedict

Gregory tells several stories that have to do with the goods of the monastery. In the Benedictine community, all goods were held in common, and Benedict urged the monks to be good stewards of all their material resources. One story tells of a monk who attempts to claim something as his own, rather than make it available to the community for use wherever needed. One day Abbot Benedict had sent him to a nearby village to give a spiritual conference to a group of nuns. Before he left the nuns,

> they presented the monk with a few handkerchiefs, which he accepted and hid away in his habit. As soon as he got back to the abbey he received a stern reproof. "How is it,"

the abbot asked him, "that evil has found its way into your heart?" Taken completely by surprise, the monk did not understand why he was being rebuked, for he had entirely forgotten about the handkerchiefs. "Was I not present," the saint continued, "when you accepted those handkerchiefs from the handmaids of God and hid them away in your habit?" The offender instantly fell at Benedict's feet, confessed his fault and gave up the present he had received. (*Dialogues*, pp. 45–46)

While the monks shared resources and took care of what they had, hard times drew them to rely on God's providence. This story illustrates Benedict's dependence on God for all his needs and those of the monastery.

During a time of famine the severe shortage of food was causing a great deal of suffering in Campania. At Benedict's monastery the entire grain supply had been used up and nearly all the bread was gone as well. In fact, when mealtime came, only five loaves could be found to set before the community. Noticing how downcast they were, the saint gently reproved them for their lack of trust in God and at the same time tried to raise their dejected spirits with a comforting assurance. "Why are you so depressed at the lack of bread?" he asked. "What if today there is only a little? Tomorrow you will have more than you need."

The next day about thirty hundredweights of flour were found in sacks at the gate of the monastery, but no one ever discovered whose services almighty God had employed in bringing them there. When they saw what had happened, the monks were filled with gratitude and learned from this miracle that even in their hour of need they must not lose faith in the bountiful goodness of God. (*Dialogues*, pp. 47–48)

Pause: Reflect on your attitude about the things you call your own, the things you need, and the things you want. Are you careful or careless, trusting or anxious, grasping or generous, grateful or dissatisfied?

Benedict's Words

The goods of the monastery, that is, its tools, clothing or anything else, should be entrusted to [those] whom the abbot appoints and in whose manner of life he has confidence. He will, as he sees fit, issue to them the various articles to be cared for and collected after use.

Whoever fails to keep the things belonging to the monastery clean or treats them carelessly should be reproved. (*Rule*, 32.1–2,4)

For their needs, they are to look to the father of the monastery, and are not allowed anything which the abbot has not given or permitted. *All things should be the common possession* of all, as it is written, *so that no one* presumes to *call anything his own* (Acts 4:32). (*Rule*, 33.5–6)

It is written: *Distribution was made to each one as he had need* (Acts 4:35). By this we do not imply that there should be favoritism—God forbid—but rather consideration for weaknesses. Whoever needs less should thank God and not be distressed, but whoever needs more should feel humble because of his weakness, not self-important because of the kindness shown him. In this way all the members will be at peace. (*Rule,* 34.1–5)

Reflection

Those who see creation as a sacrament, a sign of God's presence, respond with respect and care for material goods, values expressed often throughout the *Rule of Benedict*. Treating everything with respect, even the most ordinary tools used in our daily work, is a way of showing reverence for the Creator of all things.

God in Christ touches us through and in the material world. The material world is given to us by God to share for our mutual joy and benefit. Benedict and his community held all property in common, with each member receiving whatever was necessary for life and work. Depending on the abbot and community for their needs expressed the monks' trust in God.

Holding all things in common like the early Christian community in the Acts of the Apostles, Benedictine monastics showed by their lives that all are one in Christ. Though all Christians are not expected to give up private ownership, we are called to recognize that the gift of creation is for the common good, to pray and work for the just distribution of the world's goods, and to be generous in sharing what we have for our use. Material expressions of love of neighbor are the natural overflow of love of God.

Engaging with the material world out of a trusting relationship with God is a much different experience than approaching it as if we are on our own, compelled to compete and dominate. A frantic pursuit of material goods, in fact, increases our sense of being separated from God, ourselves, and others. The cure for our insecurity is not the accumulation of material goods, but trust in God.

✧ Reread the first story in the "About Benedict" section. Reflect on the things you have that are important to you. Is there anything you are quietly hoarding for yourself that could better be used in the service of others? If so, ask God for the light to see how you might best share this, and for the courage to do so. If not, thank God for the grace of simplicity and generosity, and pray that through the divine mercy these qualities in you may be confirmed and increased.

✧ Reread the second story in the "About Benedict" section. Then do a ruthlessly honest reflection on this question: How much do I worry about money? Follow that with thanking God for all that you have. Then repeat slowly again and again the sentence: "In my hour of need I will not lose faith in your bountiful goodness, O God."

✧ Reread the "Benedict's Words" section. Think about the things that you have. Are there any that you have been neglecting or treating carelessly? Select one of these. Go to it now, and then begin its rehabilitation by cleaning or repairing it, or seeing to its restoration. If it has completed its days of useful service, dispose of it with gratitude.

✧ Clean out your closet, files, or workroom. Dispose of the things that you no longer need, perhaps by making them available to others who do. Before you begin, prepare yourself by praying Psalm 23, the Good Shepherd psalm, several times quite slowly. Approach your task quietly and calmly, as a process that has its own importance. While you putter, select, weed out, and reorganize, repeat over and over, "You are my shepherd, I shall not want."

✧ This week read the daily newspaper or a weekly news magazine with an eye to understanding better which people have more and which have less than they need. Before you begin your reading and after you finish it, pray sincerely and humbly for the light to know what you can do to help, and for the courage to act on your convictions.

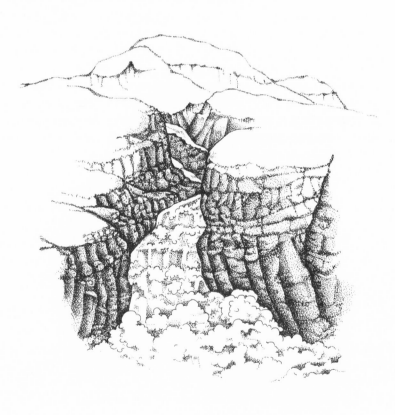

God's Word

"I tell you, do not worry about your life, what you will eat or what you will drink, or about your body, what you will wear. Is not life more than food, and the body more than clothing? . . . Why do you worry about clothing? Consider the lilies of the field, how they grow; they neither toil nor spin, yet I tell you, even Solomon in all his glory was not clothed like one of these. But if God so clothes the grass of the field, which is alive today and tomorrow is thrown into the oven, will [God] not much more clothe you—you of little faith? Therefore do not worry. . . . Strive first for the [Reign] of God and . . . righteousness, and all these things will be given to you as well.

"So do not worry about tomorrow, for tomorrow will bring worries of its own. Today's trouble is enough for today."

(Matthew 6:25–34)

Closing prayer: Thank you, gracious God, for helping me appreciate the importance of the material world. Today, help me treat everything I handle as a sacred vessel, to trust more deeply in you for what I need, and to look for ways to live more justly and to share more generously what I have with others.

O God,
You Are My Shepherd

Theme: God is compassionate and merciful, responsive to us, however mysteriously, in all our needs. Benedict's life and words reveal that divine mercy reaching out to us in the faithful love of the Good Shepherd for his sheep.

Opening prayer: Merciful God, touch me during this time of prayer with your love and mercy. Through this experience, make me a channel of your mercy and compassion for others.

About Benedict

Over and over again, Gregory portrays Benedict as a merciful and compassionate person. Touched by God's love, he was able to be merciful and compassionate toward others.

Early in Benedict's vocation as monastic founder, the monks from a monastery the saint "had built . . . on the bare rocky heights" informed him about the severe hardship of "[going] down to the lake to get water for their daily needs," descending a steep and dangerous slope. "Benedict answered them with fatherly words of encouragement," and "that same night . . . he climbed to the rocky heights and prayed there for a long time." The next day he told the monks "'that almighty God has the power to bring forth water even from that rocky summit and in His goodness relieve you of the hardship of such a long climb'" (*Dialogues*, pp. 18–19). And God did!

Gregory says that when the monks went and found the place that Benedict described as having water:

> they noticed that the surface was already moist. As soon as they had dug the ground away, water filled the hollow and welled up in such abundance that today a full stream is still flowing down from the top of the mountain into the ravine below. (*Dialogues*, p. 19)

Benedict had compassion even for his enemies. The jealous priest, Florentius, tried to kill him with a loaf of poisoned bread, and finally, through his bitter jealousy and destructive actions, drove Benedict and the monks away. Benedict did not rejoice when he heard of the accidental death of his enemy. In fact, "Benedict was overcome with sorrow and regret on hearing this" (*Dialogues*, p. 25).

Benedict cared for his brother monks from the heart. To illustrate Benedict's powerful compassion, Gregory tells of one of Benedict's miraculous healings with a story closely paralleling many of the healing stories from the Gospels.

> [The monks] were working on one of the walls that had to be built a little higher. . . . The Devil appeared to [Benedict] and remarked sarcastically that he was on his way to visit the brethren at their work. Benedict quickly sent them word to be on their guard against the evil spirit who would soon be with them. Just as they received his warning, the Devil overturned the wall, crushing under its ruins the body of a very young monk who was the son of a tax collector.
>
> Unconcerned about the damaged wall in their grief and dismay over the loss of their brother, the monks hurried to Abbot Benedict to let him know of the dreadful accident. He told them to bring the mangled body to his room. It had to be carried in on a blanket, for the wall had not only broken the boy's arms and legs but had crushed

all the bones in his body. The saint had the remains placed on the reed matting where he used to pray and after that told them all to leave. Then he closed the door and knelt down to offer his most earnest prayers to God. That very hour, to the astonishment of all, he sent the boy back to his work as sound and healthy as he had been before. (*Dialogues*, pp. 76–77)

Pause: Reflect on a time when you have experienced Christ's compassion either directly or through the compassionate response of another human person to your physical, emotional, or spiritual needs.

Benedict's Words

Benedict composed the Rule so that compassion would guide the relationships in the monastery, beginning with the abbot. He exhorts the abbot, who "is believed to hold the place of Christ in the monastery" in a special way (*Rule*, 2.2), to have compassion especially for sinners.

> The abbot must exercise the utmost care and concern for wayward brothers, because *it is not the healthy who need a physician, but the sick* (Matt 9:12). Therefore, he ought to use every skill of a wise physician and send in *senpectae*, that is, mature and wise brothers who, under the cloak of secrecy, may support the wavering brother, urge him to be humble as a way of making satisfaction, and *console him lest he be overwhelmed by excessive sorrow* (2 Cor 2:7). Rather, as the Apostle also says: *Let love for him be reaffirmed* (2 Cor 2:8), and let all pray for him.
>
> It is the abbot's responsibility to have great concern and to act with all speed, discernment and diligence in order not to lose any of the sheep entrusted to him. He should realize that he has undertaken care of the sick, not tyranny over the healthy. . . . He is to imitate the loving example of the Good Shepherd who left the ninety-nine sheep in the mountains and went in search of the one sheep that had strayed. So great was his compassion for its

weakness that *he* mercifully *placed it on his* sacred *shoulders* and so carried it back to the flock (Luke 15:5). (*Rule*, 27)

Reflection

God's love for us does not depend on our doing everything right or on our always feeling or being strong physically, emotionally, or spiritually. Experiencing our own weakness and sinfulness helps open us to divine mercy, God's loving acceptance and care for us when we are most vulnerable.

Often God's mercy touches us through someone else's compassion for us. When a "mature and wise person," perhaps a friend, a spouse, a nurse, a counselor, or a spiritual guide has the capacity to feel with us in our weakness in a way that is not condescending but respects our dignity, the balm of God's mercy can heal the wounds of our body and soul. When by a sensitive word or look someone lets us know they have some understanding of what we are going through, we can let down the defenses with which we try to hide our weakness from ourselves and others. We begin to be aware of God's presence welling up through our weaknesses like healing oil.

Sometimes God's mercy floods us directly from within, giving us the capacity to be kind to ourselves, to silence the harsh voice of that inner critic for whom our performance in life never seems adequate. We hear God's voice from inside, saying, "I know you; I love you just as you are. I will be your strength and consolation. My mercy, not your own strength, will save you."

Whether from within or through others, Christ's mercy and compassion are always with us to heal, forgive, strengthen, and console. Christ the Physician is always here for those who need healing, that is, all of us! Christ the Good Shepherd is always looking for the one who is lost!

✧ Think about a recent time in your life, when you were in a great deal of pain—physical, emotional, or spiritual—and someone was with you in a way that brought you home to a deeper wholeness and peace.

Reread the "Benedict's Words" section. In light of this passage, reflect on what the person in your life said or did that consoled, renewed, or strengthened you in body and spirit. Turn to Christ, the Good Shepherd, and thank him in whatever way you wish for the compassionate way he was with you in that person.

✧ Settle down in a quiet spot and let yourself become aware of some way in which you feel lost or alone, separated from God or others. Articulate for yourself, in writing if that helps you, all the feelings and attitudes related to that experience. Make a choice to trust in God's mercy, and slowly repeat the following psalm verse over and over:

> Listen to me, O God, and answer me,
> because I am poor and afflicted.
> Save me from death, because I am loyal to you;
> save me, because I am your servant and trust in you.
> You are my God, so be merciful to me.
>
> (Psalm 86:1–3)

✧ Are there times when you have been harsh toward yourself or others because of some mistake, some sin, some physical or psychological need or weakness, or some feeling or judgment that you or they do not "measure up"? Reread the "About Benedict" section. Now call to mind one of the particular times you have despised need, weakness, or sin in yourself or another. Pray with confidence for the grace to know God's mercy so that you may extend it to yourself or the other. Relive the incident in your imagination but change your response, if you can, to one of compassion and mercy.

✧ Memorize and repeat frequently today any one or two of the following lines of Psalm 51:

> In your goodness, O God, have mercy on me;
> with gentleness wipe away my faults.
>
> (51:1)

> Once more be my savior; revive my joy.
> Strengthen and sharpen my still weak spirit.
>
> (51:12)

✦ Over the next weeks, use the Gospel of Luke for *lectio divina*. Pay special attention to the ways Christ is compassionate toward those in need, and reflect on the ways you experience his compassion in your life.

God's Word

> [O God], you are my shepherd;
> I shall not want.
> In verdant pastures you give me repose.
> Beside restful waters you lead me;
> you refresh my soul.
> You guide me in right paths
> for your name's sake.
> Even though I walk in the dark valley
> I fear no evil;
> for you are at my side.
> Your rod and your staff give me courage.
> You spread the table before me
> in the sight of my foes.
> You anoint my head with oil;
> my cup brims over.
> Only goodness and kindness follow me
> all the days of my life;
> and I shall dwell in your house
> for years to come.
>
> (Psalm 23)

Closing prayer: Merciful God, I am moved by your compassion for me even in the darkest valleys of my sin and in the deepest fears of my own weakness. Your rest has refreshed my soul, your guidance has corrected my course, and your strength has renewed my spirit. Certainty that your goodness and kindness follow me all the days of my life gives joy to my heart.

✧ **Meditation 14** ✧

Welcomed as Christ

Theme: We have the opportunity to welcome Christ hospitably in all those who come into our life daily. Invited or uninvited they come, entering our home, our office, or even on the Internet. Christ's presence in the poor person and the stranger especially calls out for our response.

Opening prayer: Gracious God, fill me now with the light and warmth of your hospitable Spirit so that I may grow more gracious and generous in my ability to receive Christ in those you send into my life.

About Benedict

Guests arrived at any time of the day or night at the gates of Benedict's monasteries: relatives of the monks, local shepherds and farmers, sick people looking for relief, poor people, the suffering, and visiting monks. Often they came hoping for something: inspiration, food, healing, help with discerning God's will, or sometimes even a chance to give something to the monastery. According to the Rule, Benedict saw Christ himself in these guests, especially in the poor, the stranger, and the pilgrim. He had taken Christ's word to heart: "*I was a stranger and you welcomed me* (Matt 25:35)" (*Rule*, 53.1).

Gregory's stories about Benedict and his often colorful guests show the kind of uniquely tailored care with which each guest was received. Gregory claims to have heard one story from Peregrinus, a disciple of Benedict, whose name in Latin actually means "stranger." Maybe Peregrinus was particularly sensitive to Benedict's treatment of strangers! According to Gregory, Peregrinus told him of a Catholic layman who was heavily burdened with debt and felt that his only hope was to disclose the full extent of his misfortune to the man of God. So he went to Benedict and explained that he was being constantly tormented by a creditor to whom he owed seventy dollars.

> "I am very sorry," the saintly abbot replied. "I do not have that much money in my possession." Then to comfort the poor man in his need, he added, "I cannot give you anything today, but come back again the day after tomorrow."
>
> In the meantime the saint devoted himself to prayer with his accustomed fervor. When the debtor returned, the monks, to their surprise, found thirteen gold pieces lying on top of a chest that was filled with grain. Benedict had the money brought down at once. "Here, take these," he told him. "Use twelve to pay your creditor and keep the thirteenth for yourself." (*Dialogues*, pp. 57–58)

Pause: What is your attitude toward the various familiar and unknown people who knock at the door of your life daily?

Benedict's Words

All guests who present themselves are to be welcomed as Christ, for he himself will say: *I was a stranger and you welcomed me* (Matt 25:35). Proper honor must be shown *to all, especially to those who share our faith* (Gal 6:10) and to pilgrims.

Once a guest has been announced, the superior and the brothers are to meet him with all the courtesy of love.

First of all, they are to pray together and thus be united in peace. . . .

All humility should be shown in addressing a guest on arrival or departure. By a bow of the head or by a complete prostration of the body, Christ is to be adored because he is indeed welcomed in them. After the guests have been received, they should be invited to pray; then the superior or an appointed brother will sit with them. The divine law is read to the guest for his instruction, and after that every kindness is shown to him. The superior may break his fast for the sake of a guest. . . . The abbot shall pour water on the hands of the guests, and the abbot with the entire community shall wash their feet. . . .

Great care and concern are to be shown in receiving poor people and pilgrims, because in them more particularly Christ is received; our very awe of the rich guarantees them special respect.

The kitchen for the abbot and guests ought to be separate, so that guests—and monasteries are never without them—need not disturb the brothers when they present themselves at unpredictable hours. Each year, two brothers who can do the work competently are to be assigned to this kitchen. Additional help should be available when needed, so that they can perform this service without grumbling. . . .

The guest quarters are to be entrusted to a God-fearing brother. Adequate bedding should be available there. The house of God should be in the care of wise men who will manage it wisely. (*Rule*, 53.1–18,21–22)

Reflection

"All are to be welcomed as Christ." The Rule repeats this point several times, with the addition of special emphasis on receiving the poor and pilgrims. The same courtesy, love, humility, and kindness with which Christ would be received is to be extended to all.

Since their spiritual needs were of primary importance, the first thing shared with guests was prayer. However, the practical details of hospitality were also to be well attended to. Guests were to be given an adequate place to sleep and served the same food that the abbot, who shared their table, received.

The community was not expected, however, to take in those whose presence would be destructive or unhealthy. Rather, Benedict said, "prayer must always precede the kiss of peace because of the delusions of the devil" (*Rule*, 53.5). Nor were community members expected to perform superhuman feats by working day and night to serve guests. Enough help was to be provided so they could serve without cause for complaint. The Rule also safeguarded the privacy and solitude necessary for the basic well-being and life of prayer that the monks needed.

Hospitality offered to strangers, acquaintances, family, and friends is a way of prayer, the expression in body and spirit of our welcome to Christ within. Some who knock at the door of our home or heart have more of a claim on our attention and response than others: perhaps those related by blood or spirit, but most especially those who are without a home and those who are poor or suffering in any way. Welcoming them warmly ends up being not only our gift to them but their gift to us, the blessing of God's mercy on us in Christ.

In order for us to extend a sincere, generous, and effective welcome to those guests that are ours to serve, without overprotecting ourselves, we need to apply Benedict's practical advice about not unduly disturbing community life. One way to do this may be to work with others, for example, family members, the parish, or local community, so that all have enough help. Another important aspect of ensuring that we extend genuine hospitality is to recognize our real physical and emotional limits, and to take adequate time for whatever unique amount of privacy, solitude, and prayer allows each of us to open our heart to others. Love in action, the physical expression of hospitality, is essential, but our receptivity of heart and spirit makes all the difference.

✧ Reread the "Benedict's Words" section. Bring to mind each of the "guests" who will be coming to your home or workplace today. Recall the name, face, and unique characteristics of each. Select one to focus on. Aware of Christ's presence in this guest, imagine your welcome following the general structure of the Rule. Offer some sign of welcome. In your imagination, pray with the guest and reflect together on some Scripture. With "every kindness," then attend in imagination to this person's physical needs or the purpose for which he or she is coming. Conclude with spontaneous conversation with Christ about this guest and your desire to be hospitable.

✧ Think about poor people or pilgrims you know either personally or through the news media. Call on God to help you be alert to ways you could welcome them as Christ into your home. Commit yourself to some action that you are inspired to take.

✧ If you are feeling so overwhelmed with involvements and work for the "guests" in your life that you are no longer able to welcome them with "the courtesy of love," review your expectations of yourself. Find ways either to let others help you or to scale down your activity so you have the amount and kind of solitude and privacy that enables you to be truly hospitable.

✧ Today, as you meet the people who knock on the door of your home, office, or heart, remember Christ and repeat interiorly the Gospel phrase Benedict quotes: "'I was a stranger and you welcomed me'" (Matthew 25:35).

God's Word

Now as they went on their way, [Jesus] entered a certain village, where a woman named Martha welcomed him into her home. She had a sister named Mary, who sat at [Jesus'] feet and listened to what he was saying. But Martha was distracted by her many tasks; so she came to him and asked, "Lord, do you not care that my sister has left me to do all the work by myself? Tell her then to help me." But [Jesus] answered her, "Martha, Martha, you are worried and distracted by many things; there is need of only one thing. Mary has chosen the better part, which will not be taken away from her." (Luke 10:38–42)

Closing prayer: Gracious God, thank you for your constant hospitality to me. Open me to Christ's presence in each guest who knocks at the door of my home or heart today. Help me to extend a sincere and warm welcome, to provide what I can to satisfy their needs, and to receive your blessing humbly and gratefully through them.

Easter Joy

Theme: Dying in Christ is the way into the fullness of life and Easter joy in his Spirit now and forever.

Opening prayer: Christ Jesus, suffering and death was your road to risen life and to sending the Spirit. Open me now to that Spirit of life and joy present within, so that I can be united with you as I die and rise today. Be with me also through the power of that same Spirit in my final hours of this life, trusting that it is the way to eternal life.

About Benedict

Gregory tells the following story of Benedict's last days, his death, and his entrance into the lasting joy of heaven:

> In the year that was to be his last, the man of God foretold the day of his holy death to a number of his disciples. In mentioning it to some who were with him in the monastery, he bound them to strict secrecy. Some others, however, who were stationed elsewhere he only informed of the special sign they would receive at the time of his death.
>
> Six days before he died he gave orders for his tomb to be opened. Almost immediately he was seized with a

violent fever that rapidly wasted his remaining energy. Each day his condition grew worse until finally on the sixth day he had his disciples carry him into the chapel, where he received the Body and Blood of our Lord to gain strength for his approaching end. Then, supporting his weakened body on the arms of his brethren, he stood with his hands raised to heaven and as he prayed breathed his last.

That day two monks, one of them at the monastery, the other some distance away, received the very same revelation. They both saw a magnificent road covered with rich carpeting and glittering with thousands of lights. From his monastery it stretched eastward in a straight line until it reached up into heaven. And there in the brightness stood a man of majestic appearance, who asked them, "Do you know who passed this way?"

"No," they replied.

"This," he told them, "is the road taken by blessed Benedict, the Lord's beloved, when he went to heaven." (*Dialogues*, pp. 74–75)

Pause: Has there been a time in your life when you have been able to entrust yourself to the Risen Christ in the midst of suffering?

Benedict's Words

The life of a monk ought to be a continuous Lent. Since few, however, have the strength for this, we urge the entire community during these days of Lent to keep its manner of life most pure and to wash away in this holy season the negligences of other times. This we can do in a fitting manner by refusing to indulge evil habits and by devoting ourselves to prayer with tears, to reading, to compunction of heart and self-denial. During these days, therefore, we will add to the usual measure of our service something by way of private prayer and abstinence from food or drink, so that each of us will have something above the assigned measure to offer God of [their] own will *with the joy of the Holy Spirit* (1 Thess 1:6). In other words, let each one deny himself some food, drink, sleep, needless talking and idle jesting, and look forward to holy Easter with joy and spiritual longing. (*Rule*, 49.1–7)

Reflection

Traditionally, Benedict's final passing through death to eternal life is celebrated on 21 March, often the first day of spring in the northern hemisphere. It always falls during the season of Lent and Easter, the church's spring. The earth rejoices. New life bursts through the death of winter. Dormant roots stretch and bend, and fallen seeds sprout into tender shoots.

During Benedict's time, life was short, and death a constant companion. Just as Christ reminded his disciples to be ready like the bride waiting for the bridegroom, Benedict urged his disciples to remind themselves daily of their death and be mindful of the way they lived. On the other hand, Benedict told the monks not to give way to sadness and gloom during Lent, the season for dying to our narrowly selfish ways. Lent is rather a time to "look forward to holy Easter with joy and spiritual longing." Christ, like the Gospel "grain of wheat," was buried in the earth and died (John 12:24), only to be raised up by God in the fullness of life in the Spirit.

Easter, celebrating the Resurrection, became the central focus of the year in Benedict's monastery. It served as the pivotal point around which the seasons of fast and the seasons of celebration were organized. Easter joy not only awaits us at the end of our life on earth, but lives in us now since Christ lives on in us in his Holy Spirit, even in the midst of our suffering.

Easter life will finally transform death completely. As our way into lasting life, death is not an enemy but a friend. According to Gregory, when Benedict was about to die, he consciously united himself with Christ's dying and rising in the Eucharist. Then with hands raised, he offered himself with Christ to God as he breathed out his spirit. United with Christ, Benedict embraced his death and the fullness of heavenly life and joy. His physical disintegration opened a "magnificent road" to heaven, the eternal Easter.

✧ Think of the times today, or yesterday, that you felt like you were "dying" in some way: revealing something risky about yourself to another, listening carefully to someone when you wanted to hurry away, or carrying through on something you were afraid of. After praying to the Holy Spirit for guidance, select one of these incidents. Recall and write what happened and how you felt about it. Were you conscious of the moment you decided to leap into the unknown or unwanted? Were you aware of the inner support, the inner strength that made the choice and action possible? What was your inner response afterward?

Now consciously open yourself to Christ's presence in the event of this dying. Stand and raise your arms, if not physically at least in heart and imagination, as you offer yourself in that "death" and as you in body, soul, and spirit welcome the risen life of Christ.

✧ Think of the things that are weighing you down today: work, responsibilities, relationships, or feelings about yourself or others. Imagine yourself leaving those things just as they are for now and walking slowly, steadily, and expectantly into the center of your being where the source of joy, the Spirit of the Risen Christ, lives. Pray in whatever way attracts you, with or without words.

✧ Reread the "About Benedict" section. Notice what Benedict asked for as his death approached and what he did. Now imagine that you are going to die in six days. What would you ask for? Where would you want to be? What would you want to do? Who would you want to be with you? What interior dispositions would you want to be yours as you breathed your last? Converse with God, Christ, or the Holy Spirit about your death, asking for what you need or want, or just expressing your feelings as honestly as you can. If you can, consciously unite yourself in that future moment with Christ, lifting up your hands in offering your life and death completely to him.

✧ Reread the "Benedict's Words" section. Ask Christ how he wants you to become more open to Easter joy, the presence of his Spirit within you.

✧ Purposefully recall the suffering of your friends and associates, and the injustice, oppression, and violence going on in our cities and in various countries around the world.

If you are going to participate in the Eucharist, arrive at the place of Eucharist a little ahead of time. Quiet down in whatever way you do this most easily. Turn your attention to Christ. Recall your suffering and that of others. Make a conscious intention to entrust it all to Christ, letting it be united with his dying as it is celebrated in this Eucharist. Ask simply and humbly that this suffering lead somehow into his risen life and joy in him.

✧ Sing a favorite hymn that celebrates the Resurrection, Christ's conquering of death, and his promise of life eternal.

God's Word

The sufferings of this present time are not worth comparing with the glory about to be revealed to us. For the creation waits with eager longing for the revealing of the children of God. We know that the whole creation has been groaning in labor pains until now; and not only the creation, but we ourselves, who have the first fruits of the Spirit, groan inwardly while we wait for adoption, the redemption of our bodies. For in hope we were saved. (Romans 8:18,22–23)

Closing prayer: Christ Jesus, thank you for increasing my courage to enter into your dying and rising today. May the joy that your Spirit brings help all of us to be conscious of the life hidden in our daily deaths and the eternal life that will be our lasting reward when our earthly pilgrimage is completed.

L·IS·T·E·N

✧ For Further Reading ✧

Chittister, Joan D. *The Rule of Benedict: Insights for the Ages.* New York: Crossroad, 1993.

———. *Wisdom Distilled from the Daily: Living the Rule of St. Benedict Today.* San Francisco: HarperCollins, 1991.

de Waal, Esther. *Living with Contradiction: Reflections on the Rule of St. Benedict.* London: Fount Paperbacks, 1989.

———. *Seeking God: The Way of St. Benedict.* Collegeville, MN: Liturgical Press, 1984.

Fry, Timothy, ed., *RB 1980, The Rule of St. Benedict in English.* Collegeville, MN: Liturgical Press, 1982.

Gregory the Great. *The Life of Saint Benedict.* Commentary by Adalbert deVogüé. Translated by Hilary Costello and Eoin de Bhaldraithe. Petersham, MA: St. Bede's Publications, 1993.

Kardong, Terrence. *The Benedictines.* Wilmington, DE: Michael Glazier, 1988.

Schauble, Marilyn, and Barbara Wojciak, eds., *A Reader's Version of the Rule of Saint Benedict in Inclusive Language.* Erie, PA: Mount Saint Benedict, 1989.

Stead, Julian. *Saint Benedict: A Rule for Beginners.* Hyde Park, NY: New City Press, 1994.

Taylor, Brian C. *Spirituality for Everyday Living.* Collegeville, MN: Liturgical Press, 1989.

Acknowledgments *(continued)*

The psalms in this book are from *Psalms Anew: In Inclusive Language,* compiled by Nancy Schreck and Maureen Leach (Winona, MN: Saint Mary's Press, 1986). Copyright © 1986 by Saint Mary's Press. All rights reserved.

The scriptural material found on pages 61, 66, and 89 (second excerpt) is freely adapted and is not to be understood or used as an official translation of the Bible.

All other scriptural quotations in this book are from the New Revised Standard Version of the Bible. Copyright © 1989 by the Division of Christian Education of the National Council of the Churches of Christ in the United States of America. Used with permission. All rights reserved.

The excerpt by Adalbert de Vogüé, OSB, on page 16 is from *The Life of Saint Benedict,* by Gregory the Great, translated by Hilary Costello and Eoin de Bhaldraithe (Petersham, MA: St. Bede's Publications, 1993), page viii. Copyright © 1993 by St. Bede's Publications.

The excerpts on pages 17 (first excerpt), 17 (second excerpt), 17–18, 18 (first excerpt), 19–20, 20 (first excerpt), 21 (first excerpt), 21 (second excerpt), 22 (first excerpt), 22 (second excerpt), 23 (first excerpt), 23 (second excerpt), 26 (first excerpt), 26 (second excerpt), 26 (third excerpt), 26 (fourth excerpt), 32 (first excerpt), 32 (second excerpt), 32 (third excerpt), 32 (fourth excerpt), 36 (first excerpt), 36–37, 37 (first excerpt), 37 (second excerpt), 37 (third excerpt), 38 (first excerpt), 38 (second excerpt), 50, 62, 67–68, 79, 80 (first excerpt), 80 (second excerpt), 87 (first excerpt), 87 (second excerpt), 87 (third excerpt), 98–99, 99, 104–105, 105 (first excerpt), 105 (second excerpt), 105–106, 111, and 116–117 are from *Dialogues,* Book II, by Saint Gregory the Great, and found in *Life and Miracles of St. Benedict,* translated by Odo J. Zimmerman, OSB, and Benedict R. Avery, OSB (Westport, CT: Greenwood Press, 1980), pages 25, 25–26, 1, 2, 3, 4, 5, 8, 16, 22, 32, 74, 67–68, 68, 68, 69, 1, 2, 5, 11, 16, 17, 17, 18, 20, 20, 25–26, 63–64, 70–71, 20–22, 38, 39, 46–47, 52, 7, 11, 45–46, 47–48, 18–19, 19, 25, 76–77, 57–58, and 74–75, respectively. Copyright © 1949 by the Order of St. Benedict.

The excerpts on pages 23 (third excerpt), 27 (first excerpt), 27 (second excerpt), 27 (third excerpt), 28 (first excerpt), 28 (second excerpt), 28 (third excerpt), 29 (first excerpt), 29 (second excerpt), 29 (third excerpt), 29 (fourth excerpt), 30 (first excerpt), 30 (second excerpt), 32–33, 33 (first excerpt), 38 (third excerpt), 38 (fourth excerpt), 38 (fifth excerpt), 38 (sixth excerpt), 38 (seventh excerpt), 42, 43 (first excerpt), 43 (second excerpt), 44–45, 45 (first excerpt), 50, 51 (first excerpt), 51 (second excerpt), 56, 57 (first excerpt), 57 (second excerpt), 57–58, 58 (first excerpt), 62–63, 68–69, 69 (first excerpt), 73 (first excerpt), 73 (second excerpt), 73 (third excerpt), 73 (fourth excerpt), 74, 80, 81 (first excerpt), 81–82, 88 (first excerpt), 88 (second excerpt), 92, 93 (first excerpt), 93 (second excerpt), 93 (third excerpt), 93 (fourth excerpt), 93 (fifth excerpt), 94 (first excerpt), 94 (second excerpt), 100 (first excerpt), 100 (second excerpt), 100 (third excerpt), 106 (first excerpt), 106–107, 110, 111–112, 113, and 117–118 are from *RB 1980: The Rule of St. Benedict in Latin and English with Notes,* edited by Timothy Fry, OSB (Collegeville, MN: Liturgical Press, 1981), pages 161, 267, 161, 183, 203, 201, 187, 295, 183, 185, 283, 157, 165–167, 161, 157, 157, 159, 297, 183, 295, 203, 205, 205, 211, 243, 185, 249–251, 237, 249–251, 159, 249–251, 233–235, 157, 159, 157, 187–189, 237, 237, 255, 243, 191, 193, 201, 199–201, 187, 197, 279, 281, 233, 179–181, 181, 175–177, 209, 293–295, 229–231, 231, 231, 173, 223–225, 255–257, 255–259, 257, and 253, respectively. Copyright © 1981 by the Order of St. Benedict. Used by permission of the publisher.

The excerpt on page 65 is from the English translation of the "Exsultet" from the "Rite of Holy Week" in *The Roman Missal* (New York: Catholic Book Publishing Company, 1985), pages 178–181. Copyright © 1972 by the International Committee on English in the Liturgy. All rights reserved. Used with permission.

The excerpt on pages 86–87 is from *Dialogues,* Book III, by Saint Gregory the Great, translated by Odo J. Zimmerman, OSB (New York: Fathers of the Church, 1959), page 144. Copyright © 1959 by Fathers of the Church.

Titles in the Companions for the Journey Series

Praying with Anthony of Padua

Praying with Benedict

Praying with Catherine McAuley

Praying with Catherine of Siena

Praying with Clare of Assisi

Praying with Dominic

Praying with Dorothy Day

Praying with Elizabeth Seton

Praying with Francis of Assisi

Praying with Hildegard of Bingen

Praying with Ignatius of Loyola

Praying with John Baptist de La Salle

Praying with John of the Cross

Praying with Julian of Norwich

Praying with Louise de Marillac

Praying with Teresa of Ávila

Praying with Thérèse of Lisieux

Praying with Thomas Merton

Praying with Vincent de Paul

Order from your local religious bookstore or from

Saint Mary's Press
702 TERRACE HEIGHTS
WINONA MN 55987-1320
USA
1-800-533-8095